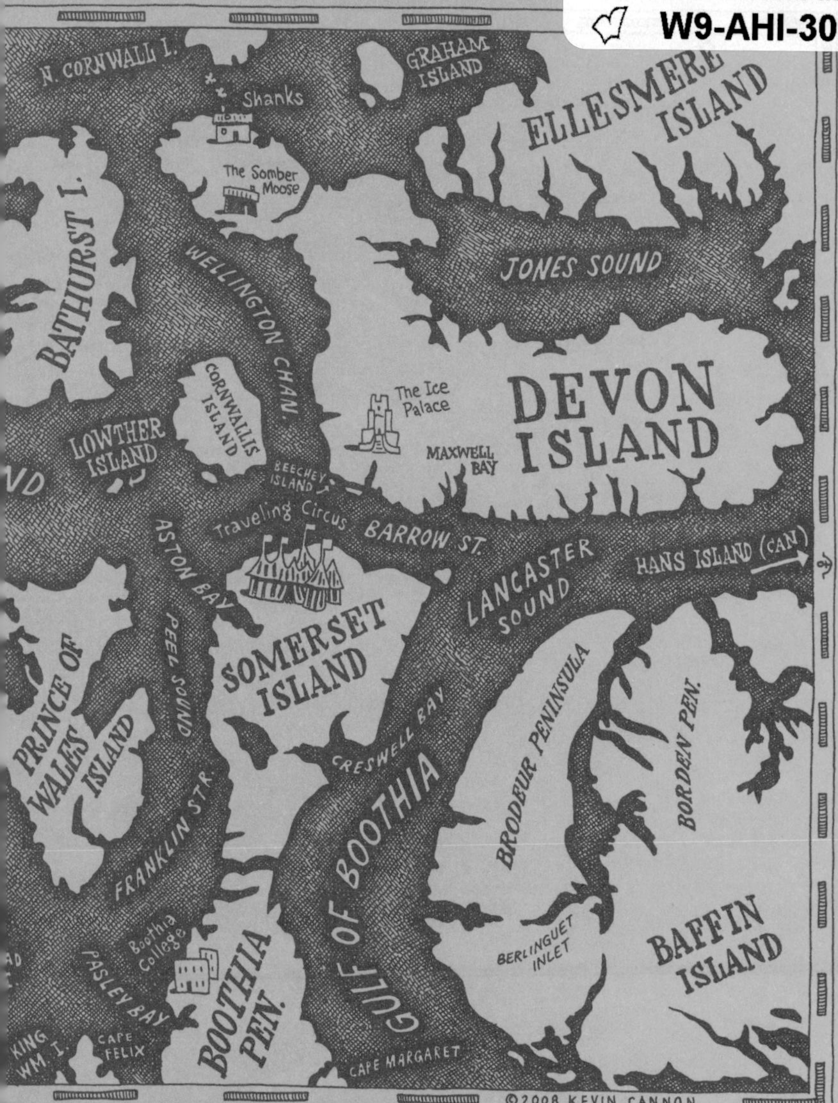
N. CORNWALL I.
GRAHAM ISLAND
Shanks
ELLESMERE ISLAND
The Somber Moose
BATHURST I.
WELLINGTON CHAN.
JONES SOUND
CORNWALLIS ISLAND
The Ice Palace
DEVON ISLAND
LOWTHER ISLAND
MAXWELL BAY
BEECHEY ISLAND
ND
Traveling Circus
BARROW ST.
ASTON BAY
LANCASTER SOUND
HANS ISLAND (CAN)
PEEL SOUND
SOMERSET ISLAND
PRINCE OF WALES ISLAND
CRESWELL BAY
BRODEUR PENINSULA
BORDEN PEN.
GULF OF BOOTHIA
FRANKLIN STR.
Boothia College
PASLEY BAY
BOOTHIA PEN.
BERLINGUET INLET
BAFFIN ISLAND
KING WM. I.
CAPE FELIX
CAPE MARGARET
©2008 KEVIN CANNON

FAR ARDEN

by Kevin Cannon

TOP SHELF PRODUCTIONS

ATLANTA / PORTLAND

ISBN 978-1-60309-036-0

1. NAUTICAL FICTION
2. GRAPHIC NOVELS

PUBLISHED BY TOP SHELF PRODUCTIONS,
P.O. BOX 1282, MARIETTA, GEORGIA
30061-1282, UNITED STATES OF AMERICA.

PUBLISHERS: BRETT WARNOCK AND CHRIS STAROS.

FIRST PRINTING, MAY 2009

PRINTED IN CHINA

FOG, AND NOTHING BUT FOG,
WHEREVER WE TURN OUR EYES.

...IT SETTLES DOWN ON THE MIND AND SPIRITS,
AND EVERYTHING BECOMES ONE UNIFORM GREY.

-- FRIDTJOF NANSEN, *FARTHEST NORTH*

I

In an abandoned whaling station on the Northwest Peninsula of Devon Island lives a man as cold and unforgiving as the arctic itself...
SHANKS
ARCTIC PIRATE
"Far Arden"

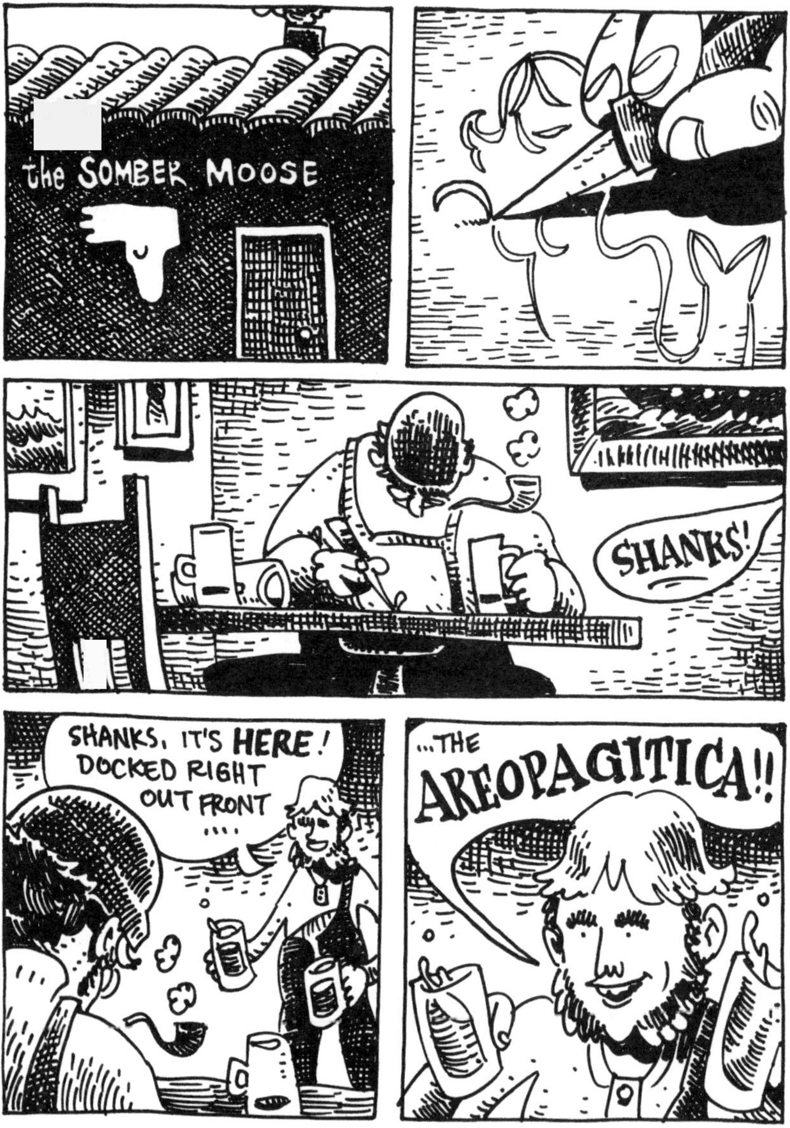
the SOMBER MOOSE
SHANKS!
SHANKS, IT'S HERE! DOCKED RIGHT OUT FRONT ....
...THE AREOPAGITICA!!

EXCELLENT.
HAFLEY, YOU KNOW... IF WE SCREW THIS UP IT WILL BE...
...the GREATEST DISASTER in the History of the WORLD

AND TO PULL THIS OFF...
...TO **RESCUE** THE AREOPAGITICA...
...WE'LL NEED TO TAKE DOWN TWO MEN IN THIS BAR.
WHO? THE GUY IN THE PITH HELMET AND THE RUSSIAN BUSINESSMAN?
NO...

THEN WHO? THE JOURNALISM STUDENTS FROM UNIVERSITY?
NO.
WHAT ABOUT THE BURLY MAN IN CHAINS AND THE CIRCUS WARDEN?
NOT THEM EITHER.
THEN WHO?
THOSE TWO. THE PLAIN-CLOTHES RCAN OFFICERS.

THEY'VE BEEN TRAILING US ALL NIGHT. WAITING FOR US TO TAKE THE BAIT.
WHAT THEY DON'T REALIZE IS THAT I CAN SMELL **RCAN** FROM A MILE AWAY...
... SINCE I USED TO BE ONE OF THEM.
SO WHAT'S THE PLAN, SHANKS? SHOULD I DRESS UP LIKE A BAKER LAKE HOOKER AND **LURE** THEM INTO THE BATHROOM WHILE YOU--
OH. THAT WORKS, TOO.

PUNCH!!!
HEADLOCK!!

Restroom

I... I THINK I NEED TO **HELP** THOSE POOR GUYS...
!!!
BOOTHIA
NO, DAVID, YOU'LL BE **TORN APART**!
BOOTHIA
Restroom
HEAVY TABLE
JUKEBOX
OKAY, Let's GET OUT of HERE!!

BER MOOSE
AREOPAGITICA
TRIAL BY ICE
CLICK!

OH, SHE'S JUST LIKE I REMEMBER HER!
AR
CAREFUL, SHANKS, THERE MAY BE RCAN ON BOARD!
YES, OF COURSE!
AREOPAG
CREAK!!!
ARMY.
FORTUNA!

FORTUNA -- I THOUGHT YOU WERE SUCKED UNDER THE SWELLS OFF THE COAST OF BOOTHIA THREE YEARS AGO!
YOU SHOULD BE MORE WORRIED ABOUT YOUR FRIEND RIGHT NOW, ARMY.
PINHO!
I THOUGHT YOU FELL TO YOUR DEATH ON THE ROCKY BANKS OF BAKER LAKE AFTER THE INFAMOUS "HANDSOME JACK" POKER SCANDAL!
NOT ONE STEP CLOSER, SHANKS, OR I'LL SLIT HIS THROAT.
YOU KNOW I'M NOT BLUFFING.

FINISH THE MISSION, SHANKS!
YOU'VE WORKED SO HARD FOR THIS -- FORGET ABOUT ME!
IT'S PRETTY SIMPLE, SHANKS. SHOW ME WHERE YOU'VE HIDDEN THE MAP...
...AND YOU AND HAFLEY WALK OUT OF HERE **ALIVE**.

I'LL COME BACK FOR YOU, HAFLEY.
LAND!
DAMMIT.

UH...
LEAP
I WANNA RIDE, TOO!
CUT!
WHO ARE YOU?
AN ORPHAN!
ALRIGHT, HOP ON.
TRIAL BY ICE

IS THIS YOUR BOAT?
BEAN
WHA..?
THAT MADMAN STOLE MY BOAT!!!
NO MORE DEAL!!!
SLAM SHUT!!
BEANS
YES.

MY NAME IS ALISTAIR CAVENDISH AND I'M AN ORPHAN!
THAT'S GREAT. WHY DON'T YOU CHECK THE HOLD AND MAKE SURE THERE'S ENOUGH FOOD TO GET US TO GLACIERVILLE.
OKAY!
BARK! BARK! BARK!
NO FOOD-- JUST STACKS AND STACKS OF PRETTY **PUPPY BLANKETS**!
BARK! BARK!
NO FOOD?
NOPE.
BARK! BARK! BARK!

Three days later...
CHIP! CHIP! CHIP! CHIP!
DAMN ICE!
FLING!!
AT LEAST I KNOW THAT AFTER ANOTHER FEW DAYS THE HUNGER WILL GO AWAY AND THEN PRE-DEATH EUPHORIA WILL SET IN
...
PUPPIES ARE WARM!

ARMY, WHAT WAS SO IMPORTANT ABOUT THAT SHIP BACK THERE? THE AR-EE-OP ONE?
HAVE YOU EVER HEARD OF FAR ARDEN?
NO.
WELL, FAR ARDEN IS A VERY SPECIAL PLACE, BUT IT'S VERY, VERY HARD TO FIND.
THERE'S SOMETHING ON THAT SHIP THAT WILL HELP ME FIND IT.
WHY DO YOU WANT TO GO THERE SO BAD?
A LONG TIME AGO A GOOD FRIEND OF MINE WENT TO FAR ARDEN AND MADE ME PROMISE TO GO TOO.
BUT THEN I GOT... DISTRACTED... AND FORGOT ABOUT MY PROMISE.

I MADE A PROMISE ONCE: TO MYSELF.
I PROMISED MYSELF THAT ONE DAY I WOULD FIND THE MAN WHO MURDERED MY FATHER THREE YEARS AGO...
...AND DESTROY HIM!
WILL YOU HELP ME, ARMY?
TELL YOU WHAT, AL-- WE GET OUT OF THIS ALIVE AND I'LL MAKE SURE WE FIND THAT BASTARD.

wake up, army.
WAKE UP ARMY, THE MEN ARE HERE
CRAP!
AL, C'MERE!
YEAH?
MAKE TWO BIG BLANKETS OUT OF THE FOX PELTS.
NOW!
GOD I HATE GUNS.
TRIAL BY ICE
YOU WANT TO **KILL** A MAN YOU SHOULD USE YOUR **FISTS**!

SO IN A LITTLE WHILE...
GOOD EVENING, MR. SHANKS. THANK YOU FOR TAKING SUCH GOOD CARE OF MY FOX PELTS.
ALLOW ME TO WELCOME YOU ABOARD HER MAJESTY'S ICEBREAKER **"END OF THE LINE"** !!!

RUN.
No!
ROUNDHOUSE!
FACE PUNCH!!!
BOO!!
HELP!!
HAR HAR!!
YOU IDIOT, HE'S AN ORPHAN!!
JUMP

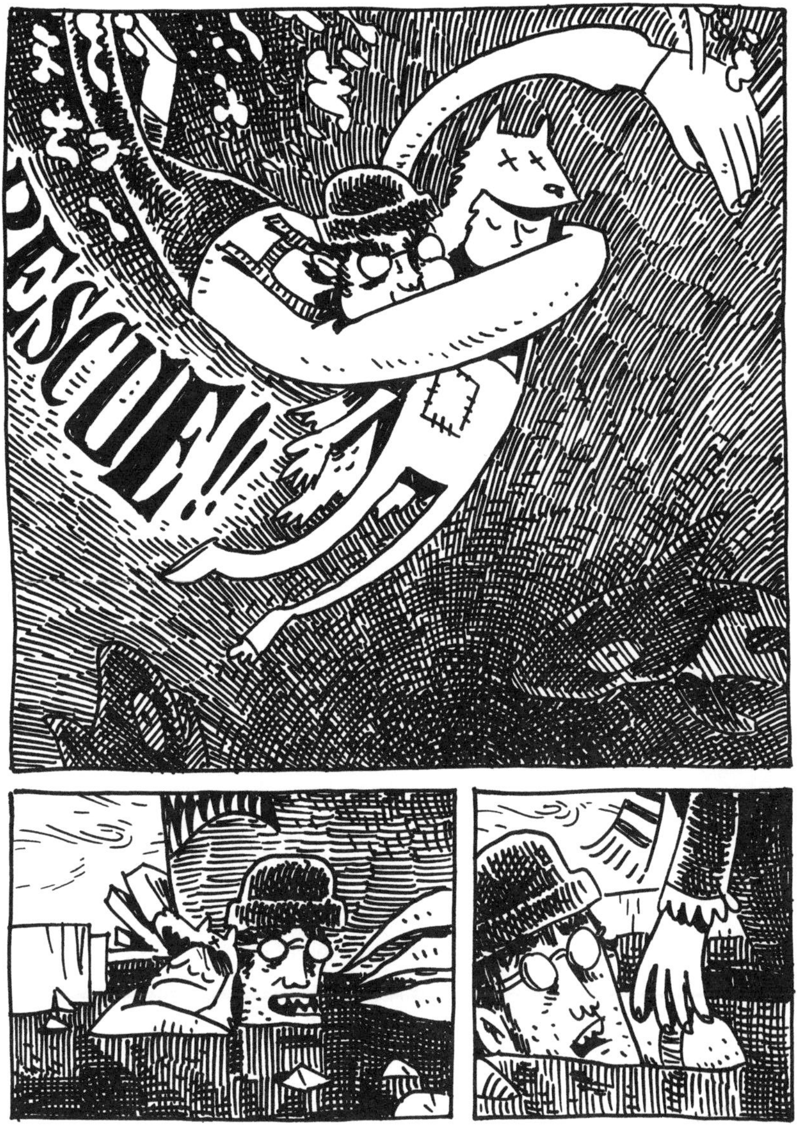
RESCUE!!

EAT EAT EAT
ARMY, WHO ARE THESE PEOPLE AND WHY DID THEY RESCUE US?
I DON'T KNOW, BUT A MEAL'S A MEAL.
ARE YOU STILL GOING TO FIND THE MAN WHO KILLED MY FATHER?
I'M GOING TO DO A LOT OF THINGS...
...I'M GOING TO AVENGE YOUR FATHER'S DEATH, FIND THE AREOPAGITICA, SAVE HAFLEY, POSSIBLY REKINDLE A ROCKY LOVE AFFAIR WITH FORTUNA (BUT PROBABLY NOT)...
...AND FULFILL MY PROMISE TO FIND FAR ARDEN, AND MEET UP WITH MY FRIEND AND MENTOR, SIMON ARCTAVIUS.

II

Meanwhile...
AREOPAGITICA
THIS WILL BE A GREAT SPOT TO HIDE OUT UNTIL SHANKS COMES TO FIND US, EH, HAFLEY?
FORTUNA-- WHERE ARE YOU GOING?
OUT.
???
BUT WE'RE IN THE MIDDLE OF NOWHERE!

BACK to SHANKS...
WE'RE ALMOST HOME, ARMY!
BEFORE WE ARRIVE, I GUESS WE SHOULD INTRODUCE OURSELVES...
BOOTHIA
MY NAME IS AMBER AND THIS IS DAVID AND WE'RE FROM--
WAIT!!
???
???

OH, MY, MY!
DAVID, POINT THE BOAT IN THE DIRECTION OF THAT TALL ROCK IN THE DISTANCE AND GO AS FAST AS YOU CAN!!
???
!
DIVE!!
PUNCH!!
SHANKS, WHAT IS THAT??
DINNER.

LATER...
YOUR BOAT SHOULD BE SAFE HERE ON THIS BEACH. THE SOMBER MOOSE IS JUST OVER THAT HILL...
MR. SHANKS.
OH NO! IT'S THE TWO PLAINCLOTHES RCAN OFFICERS!
PREPARE TO DIE!!!
SHANKS, IT'S ME!

OH HEY, BARTHIZOD REDGRAVE, THE DEVON REP-RESENTATIVE TO THE NUNAVUT COUNCIL.
WHAT ARE YOU DOING HERE?
HERE TO SEE YOU, OLD FRIEND!
HUG!!
!!!
BARTY, YOU FAKE A SEIZURE AND I'LL TAKE DOWN THOSE RCAN STOOGES!
HAR! HAR! HAR!
YOU KILL ME, SHANKS!

SOMBER MOOSE
...SO, TO REITERATE WHAT I SAID ON THE WALK OVER HERE, SAMPSON AND JOSH HERE ARE NOT NAVAL OFFICERS BUT COPS OF A SPECIAL "NATURE"...
...ENVIRONMENTAL COPS! THEY WERE GOING TO BRING DOWN THE INFAMOUS "FOX CAPTAIN" FOR POACHING ARCTIC FOX PELTS...
...BUT YOU BEAT THEM TO IT!
HERE'S THE FOX CAPTAIN...
...AND HIS SIBERIAN BUYER.

BOTH OF WHOM, THANKS TO YOU, ARE NOW UNDER CONTROL.
SAMPSON, YOU KNOW WHAT'S **NOT** UNDER CONTROL? GLOBAL WARMING.
THAT'S RIGHT, JOSH. RISING TEMPERATURES ARE HAVING VERY REAL EFFECTS HERE IN THE ARCTIC. **POLAR BEARS**, FOR INSTANCE, ARE DYING IN DROVES DUE TO A LACK OF TRAVERSABLE PACK ICE.
I'LL DRINK TO THAT! IT'S ABOUT TIME WE GOT THE UPPER HAND ON THOSE **KILLERS**!
CONSUM
CONSU
SHANKS, I'D LIKE TO INVITE YOU AND YOUR FRIENDS TO A LITTLE PARTY I'M THROWING TONIGHT ...

"WHERE YOU'LL BE **GUESTS OF HONOR**!"
YOU **CAN'T** BE SERIOUS.
AREOPAGITICA
YOU **REALLY** THINK SHE LEFT TO SEE **SHANKS**?
AFTER ALL THE CRAP HE PUT HER THROUGH THREE YEARS AGO?
TRUST ME, PINHO --
--FORTUNA WOULD RATHER BE IN A COMMITTED RELATIONSHIP WITH YOU...

"... THAN OFF SNEAKING AROUND WITH A GUY LIKE SHANKS."
WOW!!
BOOTHI
I CAN'T BELIEVE WE WERE INVITED TO THE GOVERNOR'S ICE PALACE FOR THE ECO-SUMMIT!!
WELL, DON'T GET TOO EXCITED. I CAN SMELL WHEN BARTHIZOD HAS AN AGENDA UP HIS SLEEVE.
OH MY GOD, WHAT-AM-I-GOING-TO-WEAR?!
WILL YOU STOP ACTING LIKE AN IDIOT!
BOOTHIA
THIS IS REALLY IMPORTANT TO ME!!
WE'RE CLOSE TO THE CITY, IF YOU WANT TO GO SHOPPING.

SO ANYWAY, LIKE I WAS JUST TELLING YOU, DAVID AND I ARE FRESHMEN AT BOOTHIA COLLEGE. DAVID DOESN'T KNOW WHAT HE'S DOING WITH HIS LIFE, BUT I WANT TO BE A JOURNALIST!
Marty's
AND MY FIRST ASSIGNMENT IS YOU, ARMY. THE BOOTHIA TATTLER WANTS THE DIRT ON YOUR LOVE LIFE!
WELL, UH--
OH MY GOD!
it's gorgeous!!
FANCY DRESS

DING
Marty's
HELLO THERE!
HI, HOW MUCH IS THE DRESS IN THE WINDOW?
$250
OH. UM. I HAVE TO GO TALK TO MY BOYFRIEND.
WHAT DO YOU HAVE FOR $10?

ARMY, I'M GOING TO GO TRY ON SOME DRESSES.
OKAY.
HEY MARTY. QUESTION FOR YOU ABOUT THIS BOWTIE...
CHANGING ROOM
SORRY, I HAVE TO GO IN THE BACK FOR A FEW MINUTES.
?
BLEGH.

BURST IN!
ARMY! WHAT ARE YOU
WALL PUNCH!!
OH ARMY, THANK YOU!!
ATTENTION SHOPPERS: MARTY'S IS NOW HAVING A HUGE SALE...

"...EVERYTHING IS HALF OFF."
...SO THEN WE FAKED OUR DEATHS, AND HAD TO LIVE UNDERGROUND.
WE'VE SPENT THE LAST THREE YEARS OF OUR LIVES TRYING TO FIND FAR ARDEN.
AND NOW THAT WE'RE FINALLY CLOSE TO GETTING SHANKS' MAP...
...HER INTEREST SUDDENLY UNRAVELS!
NO OFFENSE TO YOUR MARRIAGE, PINHO...
!!!

"...BUT YOU'VE GOT BIGGER FISH TO FRY."
ICE PALACE
WHAT DO YOU MEAN, I CAN'T COME IN?! I'M ON THE LIST AND I "BOUGHT" A TUX!
NOT YOU, MR. SHANKS... THE FISH.
TONITE: "ECO-SUMMIT"
OH. YEAH.
BUT IF YOU'D LIKE TO KEEP IT IN THE KITCHEN, FEEL FREE.
TO THE KITCHEN, ALISTAIR!
YIP!

OH, THIS PALACE IS SO BEAUTIFUL AND FILLED WITH SO MANY PEOPLE!
SO MANY PEOPLE!
LISTEN, AMBER, I'M SORRY I SNAPPED AT YOU OUTSIDE THE STORE.
OH, YOU'RE SWEET!
SO... DID YOU AND SHANKS HAVE A GOOD CHAT IN THE DRESSING ROOM?
WHAT IS THAT SUPPOSED to MEAN?!?

IS THERE LIKE A PAYPHONE?
BOOTHIA COLLEGE, PLEASE. PROFES-SOR EMILE BESSEHL.
HELLO, DAVID.
OH MY GOD! HOW LONG DO I HAVE TO KEEP DATING THIS GIRL??
HAS SHE GIVEN SHANKS THE LETTER?
NOT YET.
CHRIST, CAN'T I JUST GIVE IT TO HIM? SHE'S EXHAUSTING!
DAVID, REMEMBER WHAT I TOLD YOU ABOUT SHANKS. HE IS A PROFESSIONAL SKEPTIC. IT TAKES A GREAT DEAL OF THEATRE FOR HIM TO GO ALONG WITH ANYTHING. JUST GET THEM ALONE AND YOU'LL BE FINE.

SO, ALISTAIR.
YOU'VE BEEN PRETTY QUIET SINCE THE ZODIAC RIDE.
EVERYTHING OKAY?
YEAH... BUT I THINK MAYBE YOU FORGOT ABOUT LOOKING FOR THE MAN WHO KILLED MY DAD.
NO WAY!
THAT'S ALL I'VE BEEN THINKING ABOUT!
PROMISE?
KITCHE
ALISTAIR. THERE'S **NOTHING** THAT COULD DISTRACT ME FROM--

HI. ARMY.
FORtUNA!!
YOU CHANGED YOUR HAIR SINCE LAST TIME I SAW YOU.
I NEED TO TALK TO YOU, ARMY. URGENTLY.
YEAH. FORTUNA, OF COURSE.

ARMY, I NEED YOU BACK IN MY LIFE.
NO.
PLEASE, ARMY! THREE YEARS OF MARRIAGE IS KILLING ME! JUST KISS ME, ARMY!
NO! I KNOW WHEN I'M BEING HAD, FORTUNA. GO BACK TO PINHO. TELL HIM YOU TRIED YOUR BEST.
YOU DON'T UNDERSTAND, ARMY... THIS IS REAL!
LET'S GO, ALISTAIR.
ALISTAIR?
GODDAMN IT...
ALISTAIR!!

HI.
HELLO, ALISTAIR!
HAVE YOU SEEN WHAT THEY'VE GOT IN THE DINING ROOM?
HELP SAVE THE POLAR BEAR!
FACTS ABOUT POLAR BEARS

ALISTAIR!
SHANKS!
SO GLAD YOU COULD MAKE IT TO THE PARTY, SHANKS.
LET'S STEP INTO THIS DARK HALL.
LET ME GET RIGHT TO THE POINT...
...I UNDERSTAND (THROUGH SOURCES THAT I CONSIDER LEGITIMATE) THAT YOU MAY BE--OR MAY SOON BE--IN POSSESSION OF A MAP OF SOME KIND, TO...
...FAR ARDEN!
BART...
DEVON ISLANDERS FIND AND CLAIM FAR ARDEN! SHANKS, IMAGINE WHAT THAT WOULD DO FOR OUR ECONOMY, NOT TO MENTION OUR STATUS IN THE HIGH ARCTIC LEAGUE!

I'M NOT A MERCENARY, BART.
THAT'S FAIR, THAT'S FAIR... BUT CONSIDER PLANTING A DEVON FLAG IN FAR ARDEN'S THICK, NUTRIENT-RICH SOIL--
NO, BART.
I DON'T WANT TO PLAY HARDBALL, SHANKS, BUT I WANT YOU TO KNOW THAT MY SIGNATURE IS THE ONLY THING KEEPING THE ROYAL CANADIAN ARCTIC NAVY FROM RAZING THE ENTIRE NORTHWEST PENINSULA!
SCREAM
ALISTAIR!!
POWER RUN!!
PANT! PANT!

PANT! PANT! PANT! PANT!
SHIT.
PANT! PANT!

III

In another room...
THERE YOU ARE, AMBER.
THERE YOU ARE, DA-A-A-VID.
THERE'S SOME COMMOTION IN THE DINING ROOM ... DO YOU WANT TO CHECK IT OUT?
MMM... I WANT TO CHECK YOU OUT.
OH. UH... OKAY...
UNTIE!

TEAR OPEN
HOP HOP
PUNCHIN' STANCE!!
ARMY, HELP!
?
FLYING BODY PUNCH!!

HMM...
HIT HIT HIT HI
WHAT'S ON YOUR MIND, SAMPSON?
WELL, IT LOOKS TO ME THAT THIS PARTICULAR POLAR BEAR HAS AN UNUSUAL CURVE TO ITS TOP LEFT CLAW.
fig 1
SO... ARE YOU THINKING WHAT I'M THINKING?
YEP. I'M PRETTY SURE THIS IS A **SOMERSET ISLAND** POLAR BEAR, WHICH--DUE TO ITS SOCIAL ISOLATION AND PLENTIFUL SEAL MEAT IN CRESWELL BAY--HAS DEVELOPED A SPECIES-WIDE **FONDNESS** FOR THE **ARCTIC FOX**.
WHICH MEANS...
ALISTAIR! BARK LIKE A FOX AND HE'LL LET YOU GO!

BARK! BARK!
YAY!
HIT
OH NO!
CRUSH!!

Then, from out of NOWHERE...
OOF!
LOCK!
THANK YOU, ANGER. EVERYONE, THIS IS ANGER, MY MAN-BEAST.
RAISED BY POLAR BEARS, MAN-BEAST IS NOW THE MOST POPULAR SIDE-SHOW ATTRACTION AT MY ARCTIC CIRCUS (CURRENTLY IN ASTON BAY).
CHILDREN GET IN FREE...

LATER...
ARE YOU OKAY, SHANKS? A POLAR BEAR. THAT'S ROUGH. SORRY WE WEREN'T THERE SOONER.
TEE, HEE. WE **CAME** AS SOON AS WE HEARD!
MOVING ON, WE'RE ALL GLAD YOU'RE OKAY.
JUST A FEW MORE MINUTES AND I COULD'VE **TAKEN** HIM!
SPIT
I WANT TO GO TO THE **CIRCUS**!!

YOU AND DAVID AND ALISTAIR WILL HAVE TO SHARE THE BED.
THERE ARE NO EXTRA COTS OR BLANKETS OR ANYTHING.
I DON'T GET A LOT OF VISITORS.
THA'S FINE, ARMY. SORRY I'M DRUNK... TOMORROW MORNING YOU CAN TELL ME ALL ABOUT YOUR **LOVE LIFE** FOR THE **BOOTHIA TATTLER**!

SLEEP.
SLEEP.
SLEEP
Fortuna

MORNING...
ARMY-- WAKE UP!!!
IT LOOKS LIKE SOME PEOPLE BROKE IN AND DRANK THREE BOTTLES OF YOUR SCOTCH!
ARMY!
RCAN
SNORE

AFTERNOON...
NICE SHIRT.
RCAN
OH, SORRY. I TOOK THIS FROM YOUR CLOSET BE-CAUSE ALL OF MY CLOTHES SMELL LIKE ASS.
RCAN
ROYAL CANADIAN ARCTIC NAVY-- VERY IRONIC WAR-DROBE CHOICE FOR A PIRATE.
HM.
WHERE'S ALISTAIR AND YOUR BOYFRIEND?
OUT. IT'S JUST YOU AND ME HERE.

SO...
...WHY DON'T WE HAVE A SEAT AND TALK?
NO OFFENSE, AMBER, BUT I'M A LITTLE TOO HUNG-OVER TO TALK ABOUT MY **SLEEPING** HABITS.
ACTUALLY, THAT WHOLE "TATTLER" ARTICLE WAS JUST A **FRONT**.
I'M REALLY HERE TO GIVE YOU A **LETTER**...
...FROM **SIMON ARCTAVIUS**.

I LIKE LONG WALKS!
SKIP
WELL, GOOD, BECAUSE WE NEED TO GIVE AMBER PLENTY OF TIME TO ... INTERVIEW... SHANKS.
OH, LOOK. HERE'S THAT DIVE BAR. LET'S MAKE A PIT STOP.
I HAVE TO MAKE A QUICK PHONE CALL. REMEMBER THAT DEVON SAILORS ARE A MEAN BUNCH, SO KEEP A **LOW PROFILE**, OKAY?
OKAY.
BESSEHL, PLEASE.
HELLO, DAVID.
HELLO, PROFES-SOR, I--

HAS ANYONE HERE BEEN to FAR ARDEN?
!

HAR HAR
HAR HAR
HAR
KNEE SLAP
HAR HAR HAR HAR
HAR
IS THERE A PROBLEM, DAVID?
NO... NO PROBLEM... ACTUALLY, CAN YOU HANG ON FOR A MINUTE?
FAR ARDEN? THERE AIN'T NO SUCH THING!
HA HA. ARE THEY TEACHING THAT CRAP IN SCHOOLS NOW?

YOU NEED TO WAIT **OUTSIDE**, ALISTAIR.
ANGRY GRAB!
NOW HOLD ON, HOLD ON...
WE DIDN'T MEAN TO LAUGH IN THE BOY'S FACE.
IT'S JUST THAT MORE THAN A FEW OF US HERE HOLD A ... A **GRUDGE** AGAINST THAT PARTICULAR LOCALE.
SEE, IT WAS THE **MYTH** OF FAR ARDEN THAT STOLE AWAY OUR LOYAL FRIEND...
...THE GREATEST MAN TO EVER SAIL THESE ARCTIC WATERS...

"... SIMON ARCTAVIUS."
TO: ARMY SHANKS DEVON ISLAND, THE GRI PENINSULA
FROM: SIMON ARCTAVIUS
HE WAS MY SAILING COACH AND HISTORY TEACHER WAY BACK AT THE ACADEMY.
THE ONLY PERSON THERE WHO TREATED ME LIKE AN ADULT.
HE HELPED ME ENLIST IN **RCAN** (WHICH WAS A VENERABLE INSTITUTION BACK THEN, NOT LIKE THE WHOREHOUSE YOU SEE TODAY).
RCAN
HE CONTINUED TO MENTOR ME AS I ROSE THROUGH THE RANKS...
...AND EVEN PICKED ME AS A **RIG HAND** ON THE **MELVILLE** DURING THE BATTLE OF LOWTHER ISLAND.

WHEN THE BUREAUCRATS TOOK OVER RCAN WE WERE THE ONLY TWO TO STAY TRUE TO THE RESISTANCE.
RCAN EXILED US TO EGLINTON ISLAND, LEAVING US FOR DEAD...
...BUT WE SURVIVED THREE WINTERS AND BUILT THE AREOPAGITICA USING AN ULU I STOLE FROM THE RCAN GALLEY.
AFTER A YEAR BACK IN CIVILIZATION HE LEFT FOR FAR ARDEN AND MADE ME PROMISE TO FOLLOW HIM IN THE AREOPAGITICA.
HANDSHAKE!!
BUT THEN FATE STEPPED IN AND I FORGOT ABOUT MY PROMISE.
WHICH IS WHY I THINK THIS LETTER MIGHT BE A PRETTY PIECE OF HATE MAIL.

WAIT, WHY WOULD AN EXPERIENCED SAILOR GO AFTER SOMETHING THAT DOESN'T EXIST?
BUT FAR ARDEN IS REAL!
WHY DOES ANYBODY BELIEVE ANYTHING? WE'RE ALL LONELY AND DEPRESSED UP HERE IN NUNAVUT.
IT'S EITHER BELIEVE IN A MAGIC FAIRY-TALE ISLAND OF LUSH FRUIT AND LONG-HAIRED TOPLESS GIRLS...
...OR DRINK.

BUT I KNOW IT'S REAL!
TUC
OKAY, FOR THE SAKE OF ARGUMENT, THERE HAVE TO BE SOME PEOPLE WHO CLAIM TO HAVE ACTUALLY BEEN THERE.
BOOTHIA
SURE. YOU WANT TO TALK TO KINCAID. HE'S RIGHT OVER THERE.
JUST DO ME A FAVOR, KID. IF HE GETS RILED UP, DON'T LET HIM GO OUTSIDE.
HUH? OH, YEAH. SURE.

SO... WE HEAR YOU'VE BEEN TO FAR ARDEN?
IT WAS A DAY... JUST LIKE TODAY...
...I WAS A SMALL-TIME FISHERMAN... JUST ME AND MY SON...
...THE FOG SETTLED LIKE A BLANKET... AND THEN A GOLD-COLORED NARWHAL SURFACED BEFORE MY BOAT...
...I FOLLOWED HIM FOR THREE DAYS... THROUGH A HUNDRED TINY INLETS...
...WHEN THE FOG LIFTED, THE NARWHAL DISAPPEARED... AND WE STOOD BEFORE AN ISLAND...

...MY SON AND I STEPPED FOOT ON HER WEIRD AND TRAGIC SHORE...
...WE CLIMBED A RIDGE AND SAW THE HEART OF FAR ARDEN -- AN UNENDING EXPANSE OF FRUIT TREES, EXOTIC FLOWERS, AND WATERFALLS...
...WE RAN DOWN TO THE BASIN AND SUNK OUR HANDS IN THE BLACK, WARM SOIL...
...THEN BEAUTIFUL WOMEN CAME AND TOOK AWAY MY SON...
...AND GREAT NORSE MEN CHASED ME OFF THE ISLAND...
...I ESCAPED... AND MY SMALL BOAT DRIFTED BACK TO DEVON.

WOW!
SO, WATCH OUT FOR BIG RED-HEADED GUYS. GOT IT.
YOU DON'T... UNDERSTAND... ...I... WAS THERE!
HOLD THE PHONE, BUDDY, I --
OH CRAP!
HELLO? HELLO? PROFESSOR BESSEHL? ... DAMN IT!
WALK TOWARD DOOR
SCREAM

WELL, HERE WE GO...
RCA
OPEN
REVEAL
QUINT
WHAT DOES IT SAY??
RCAN

"I HAVE NO EFFING IDEA."
AUG
GAUAUUGAA
UCUCAUGCU
AAUAAAUCC
GACAUCGAG
UAA

IV

Meanwhile, on the other side of the peninsula...
ALRIGHT, ANGER, LET'S FINISH LOADING UP AND THEN HEAD BACK TO ASTON BAY...
ARCTIC CIRCUS
...WHICH IS WHERE MY TRAVELING CIRCUS IS CURRENTLY LOCATED.
AS YOU KNOW.
ARCTIC CIRCUS
--WHAT THE DEVIL WAS THAT?

SOMBER
OSE
GIT HIM BACK INSIDE!
?
?
SCREAM
BLISTER
BLISTE
OH, DEAR!
DRAG INSI

HMM.
SAY...
THE SOMBER MOOSE
...WHAT'S A LITTLE GUY LIKE YOU DOING IN A ROUGH & TUMBLE PLACE LIKE DEVON?
AREN'T YOUR PARENTS AROUND?

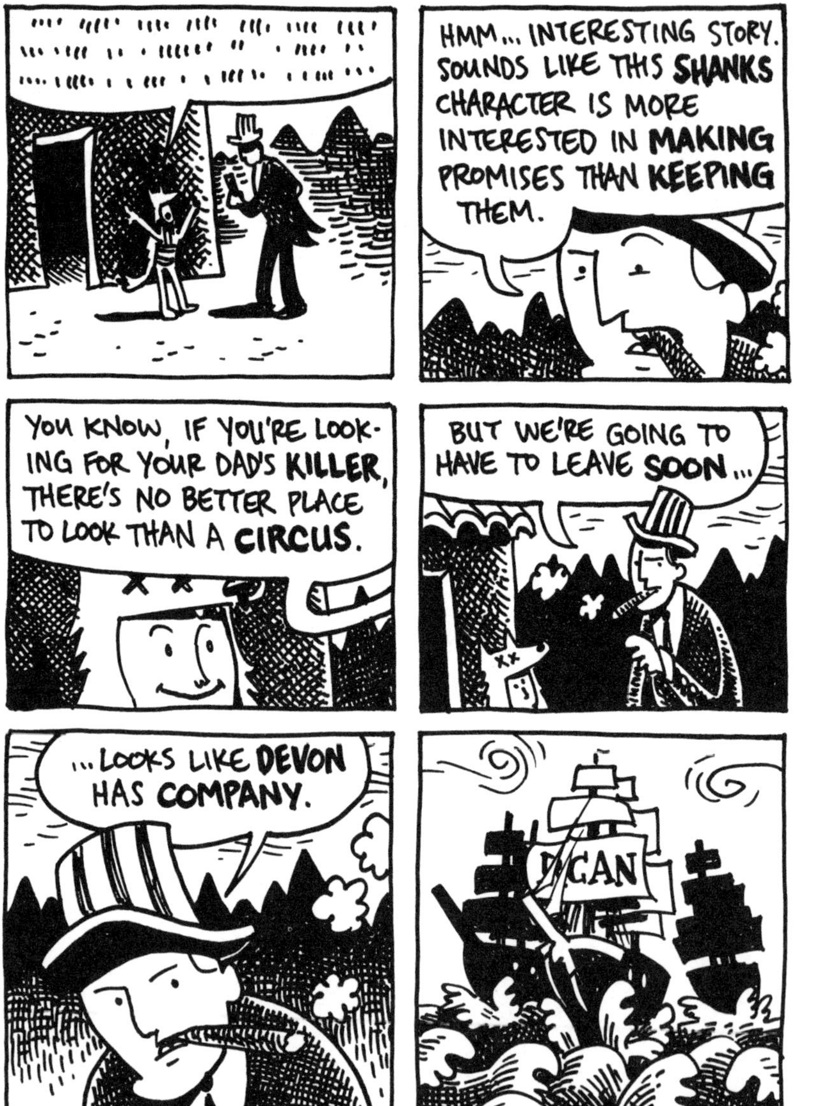
HMM... INTERESTING STORY. SOUNDS LIKE THIS SHANKS CHARACTER IS MORE INTERESTED IN MAKING PROMISES THAN KEEPING THEM.
YOU KNOW, IF YOU'RE LOOKING FOR YOUR DAD'S KILLER, THERE'S NO BETTER PLACE TO LOOK THAN A CIRCUS.
BUT WE'RE GOING TO HAVE TO LEAVE SOON...
...LOOKS LIKE DEVON HAS COMPANY.

IN THE BAR:
I TOLD YOU NOT TO LET HIM GO OUTSIDE!!
WHAT HAPPENED TO HIM?
BOOTHIA
SNOW BLINDNESS.
SOME MEN HAVE SENSITIVE EYES. IF THEY GO OUTSIDE TOO FAST... INTO THE GLARE OF THE SNOW AND THE ICE...
GROAN...
BARKEEP! WE HAVE A PROBLEM!
...RCAN!

Meanwhile, on the Areopagitica...
GEE, HAFLEY, IF I WAS SHANKS, AND MY BEST FRIEND WAS TAKEN HOSTAGE ...
...I'D HAVE TRIED TO RESCUE HIM BY NOW!
SHANKS IS COMING, PINHO. IT'S JUST A MATTER OF TIME.
YOU KNOW, IT DOESN'T HELP THAT YOU HID THE SHIP IN THIS SECRET INLET IN ASTON BAY (NEAR THE CIRCUS).
OH, THAT'S RIGHT... I FORGOT ABOUT MY PART OF THE PLAN WHERE I MAKE YOU WRITE A LETTER TO SHANKS IN ORDER TO LURE HIM TO THIS LOCATION.
BUT NOW I'M ALL TIED UP. OH, WELL. SINCE SHANKS IS SUCH A GOOD FRIEND OF YOURS, I'M SURE HE'LL BE HERE IN NO TIME.

Back on the Devon peninsula, at Shanks' house...
HMM...
"UAA" IS A COLLEGE IN THE STATES... MAYBE THAT'S A CLUE...
ARMY!
YOU'RE NOT EVEN LOOKING AT THE CODE!

SIMON ARCTAVIUS NEVER WROTE CODES LIKE THIS.
THE PUZZLES HE ENJOYED WERE GEOGRAPHIC ONES...
... TIDAL PATTERNS ... TEMPERATURE ANOMALIES...
I CAN'T HELP BUT THINK, WHAT IF HE'S BEING HELD CAPTIVE ON FAR ARDEN...
... AND THIS RANDOM SERIES OF A'S AND G'S AND U'S AND C'S IS A WARNING...
A WARNING ABOUT FAR ARDEN!
RCAN

OR... MAYBE IT'S NOTHING MORE THAN A FRIENDLY, CLEVER, "HELLO."
WELL, WHILE YOU'RE STARING INTO THE STOVE, I'M GOING TO FIGURE THIS CODE OUT.
HAND ME MY BOOK BAG SO I CAN GET SOME SCRATCH PAPER.
WHOOPS... HEY, WHAT'S THIS?
LETTER to an ARCTIC NATION
SALZAN FLUE
JUST A BOOK ABOUT GLOBAL WARMING.
HEY! THAT'S A LIBRARY BOOK!
RIP!

Back at the bar...
RCAN ATTACK!

SOMBER MOOSE
I DON'T UNDER-STAND!
OOOH
WHY IS THE NAVY ATTACKING A BAR?
THEY'RE AFTER SHANKS, NO DOUBT.
BUT DON'T WORRY. AS SOON AS THEY REALIZE SHANKS ISN'T HERE, THEY'LL SAIL OFF AND ATTACK HIM AT HIS HOUSE.
DAVID?
OOOOOH

ARMY!
I CAN'T BELIEVE YOU JUST RIPPED THAT BIO PAGE OF SALZAN FLUE RIGHT OUT OF MY BOOK!
FOLD!
DO YOU KNOW HOW MANY FINES I'LL HAVE TO PAY TO THE BOOTHIA COLLEGE LIBRARY?
TUCK!
JUST ONE, I HOPE.
RCAN
WELL... YES! AND IT WILL BE A VERY STEEP ONE AT THAT—
DID YOU HEAR SOMETHING?

BREAK THROUGH!
KICK OPEN!
ARMY!
ACK!
AMBER, GO GRAB MY SWORD! IT'S IN A LOCKBOX IN THE CABINET ABOVE THE SINK! THE COMBINATION IS RIGHT TWENTY-SEVEN, LEFT EIGHT--
DOOF!!
RCAN
PUNCH
ARMY!
NEVER MIND, AMBER, JUST GRAB THE ONE ABOVE THE TOILET!
RCAN

PREPARE...
AN
PLEASE Return me.
OH No!
PUNC ONE!
SHANKS, I--
OH SHIT! THE CODE!
ACAN
UNCH TW
HIDE!!
ROLL OF TAPE

Concurrently, on the Areopagitica...
AREOPA
WHAT THE HELL ?!?
A) WHAT HAPPENED TO THE GANGPLANK, B) WHO RAISED THE FORESAILS, AND C) HOW THE HELL DID YOU GET YOURSELF TIED UP?
I PULLED UP THE GANGPLANK, FORTUNA. IT WAS MAKING THIS IRRITATING BANGING SOUND WHENEVER THE SHIP--
SHUT UP, HAFLEY.
YES, FORTUNA.

And then, halfway between the bar and Shanks' house...
RUN RUN RUN RUN R
OH, SHIT--ALISTAIR!
UHH....
SORRY, ALISTAIR...

MISS!
WHUMP
SMAS
PUNCH PREPARATION
STOP!!

RCAN
RCAN
RCAN
RCAN
WHA--
BARTY-- YOU'RE BEHIND ALL THIS RCAN BULLSHIT?

WHAT THE HELL ARE YOU DOING, BARTY? YOU'RE A PUBLIC OFFICIAL!
AND YOU, SHANKS, POACHED AN ENDANGERED FISH. THE PROOF OF WHICH IS SITTING IN MY KITCHEN IN THE ICE PALACE.
... THUS GIVING ME JUST CAUSE TO HIRE THE ROYAL CANADIAN ARCTIC NAVY TO DETAIN YOU.
AND FOR WHAT, BARTY?
RCAN
I TRIED TO REASON WITH YOU, SHANKS, BUT THAT DIDN'T WORK. SO NOW I HAVE TO USE FORCE.
I WANT THE MAP TO FAR ARDEN, SHANKS.
TELL ME WHERE IT IS.

FINALLY!
SHANKS!
RU
OH, CRAP!
RCAN!
UH....
CRAN
PROFESSOR BESSEHL, PLEASE.

WHAT KIND OF KNOT IS THIS, HAFLEY? IT LOOKS LIKE A THIRD GRADER TIED IT.
IT'S JUST A... AN OLD FASHIONED SAILOR'S KNOT.
SPOT ME WHILE I WALK ONTO THE BOWSPRIT, WILL YOU? I NEED TO TAKE THESE FORESAILS DOWN OR WE'LL END UP ON SHORE.
SO... DID YOU HAVE A GOOD TRIP?
AND WHAT IS THAT SUPPOSED TO MEAN?
NOTHING. IT'S JUST FUNNY THAT YOU DIS-APPEAR RIGHT AFTER OUR ENCOUNTER WITH SHANKS.
YOU'RE A BASTARD, PINHO.

...YEAH, THERE'S RCAN EVERYWHERE. I'M GUESSING HE WAS TAKEN ABOARD THEIR MAIN SHIP.
IS THERE ANY WAY TO, LIKE, PRETEND TO BE RCAN?
OKAY ... OKAY ... UH-HUH.
OH, CAN YOU HANG ON A MINUTE?
CRANK
OKAY, SAY THAT LAST PART AGAIN...

A
CLEAR THROA
BEAT BEAT
RCAN

I'LL NEVER GIVE YOU THE MAP, BARTY!
NICE TRY, SHANKS.
OH, BY THE WAY, I JUST REMEMBERED SOMETHING.
ACCORDING TO A NEW DEVON ISLAND LAW, IT'S ILLEGAL FOR CIVILIANS TO WEAR RCAN CLOTHING.
SO WE'RE GOING TO HAVE TO CONFISCATE THAT SHIRT, MISS.
RCAN
ARMY!!!
GASP!
RCAN

V

LOOK! SHE'S GOT THE MAP TO FAR ARDEN TAPED TO HER STOMACH!
GET IT!
RCAN
NO! IT'S JUST SOME STUPID CODE!
ARMY! HELP!
RCAN
FACE KICK!
AGONY!!
SLICE!!

DAMMIT.
GET THE MAP, YOU FOOL!
WHA--?
SHANKS! AMBER!
KICK!
!
HIT!
FOLLOW ME, DAVID, AND GRAB YOUR GIRLFRIEND!
JUMP!

SOON...
WOW, GOOD THING THIS BOAT WAS RIGHT OUTSIDE THE WINDOW.
RCAN
EH, AMBER? AMBER?
Cold... so... cold...
BOOTHIA
WELL, MAYBE YOU SHOULD HAVE THOUGHT ABOUT THAT BEFORE WEARING AN RCAN SHIRT!
CHATTER
DAVID, TAKE THE RUDDER. AMBER, COME HERE.
OKAY... JUST SLIP IN LIKE THAT... NO, KEEP YOUR ARMS IN...
BOOTHIA
THERE. BETTER?

"YES... MUCH BETTER."
ohh...
DAMN YOU, SHANKS...
...YOU SELFISH BASTARD.
B.R.

WILL YOU PUT THAT AWAY, PINHO?
A.P.
YOU'RE SUPPOSED TO BE SPOTTING ME!
AREOPAGITICA
STOP BEING SO PISSY, FORTUNA.
MAYBE I WOULDN'T BE PISSY IF SOMEONE HADN'T HIDDEN THIS HEAP RIGHT NEXT TO A TRAVELING CIRCUS!
COULD YOU TWO PLEASE STOP BICKERING??
I CAN'T HANDLE IT!!
ONE MORE PEEP OUT OF YOU, HAFLEY, AND YOU'RE GOING IN THE HOLD!

Meanwhile, Shanks, David, and Amber sail aimlessly through loose pack ice...
OH NO -- WE FORGOT ALISTAIR!
HE DISAPPEARED AT THE...
...ON OUR WALK.
wKICK

DON'T WORRY ABOUT ALISTAIR. HE HAS STRONG BLOOD.
BLOOD! THAT'S IT! THE CODE FROM SIMON ARCTAVIUS IS WRITTEN IN THE LANGUAGE OF DNA!
I HIGHLY DOUBT THAT--
THINK ABOUT IT! SIMON IS COMMUNICATING USING SOMETHING HE KNOWS-- SCIENCE!
I JUST THOUGHT OF SOMETHING ELSE -- DAVID HAS A PROFESSOR WHO'S A NEUROSCIENTIST! I BET HE COULD DECODE THE MESSAGE!
HUH.

YOU KNOW, THAT'S NOT A HALF-BAD IDEA, AMBER. MY PROFESSOR COULD TELL YOU EXACTLY WHAT THE CODE MEANS, I'M SURE.
AND SINCE WE'RE NOT REALLY HEADED ANYWHERE, IN PARTICULAR, WE MIGHT AS WELL GO TO BOOTHIA COLLEGE--
HEY, NOW I JUST THOUGHT OF SOMETHING.
THIS BIOGRAPHY OF SALZAN FLUE THE ENVIRONMENTAL-IST THAT I RIPPED OUT OF YOUR LIBRARY BOOK--DO YOU REMEMBER THAT INCIDENT?
VAGUELY.
WELL, I TOOK IT BECAUSE I'VE BEEN MEANING TO SEE FLUE--TO ASK HIM WHEN I CAN EXPECT ALL THESE DAMN POLAR BEARS TO BE GONE.
...AND I REMEMBERED READING RECENTLY THAT FLUE IS SPENDING THIS SEASON WITH THE TRAVELING CIRCUS--GIVING LECTURES TO PROMOTE HIS BOOK.
SALZAN FLUE

...AND IT JUST SO HAPPENS THAT WE'RE NEAR ASTON BAY, WHERE THE CIRCUS IS.
SO LET'S SCRAP DAVID'S PLAN, AND GO SEE IF THIS SCIENTIST SALZAN FLUE CAN DECODE THE DNA.
YAY! GOOD IDEA, ARMY!
I REALLY THINK THAT'S A BAD IDEA--
SHIT.
WHAT?
LOOKS LIKE YOU'RE IN LUCK, DAVID...
...THE PACK ICE HAS CLOSED. WE'LL NEVER MAKE IT TO ASTON BAY.
GEE, THAT'S TOO BAD. I GUESS WE SHOULD TURN AROUND AND HEAD TO BOOTHIA COLLEGE.

BUT SOON
ARMY, WHAT ARE YOU DOING?
CLIMB!
RCAN
JUST AS I SUSPECTED. THERE'S OPEN WATER A FEW HUNDRED METERS AWAY.
IF I CAN JUMP FROM THIS GREAT HEIGHT AND STRIKE THE ICE AT THAT IMAGINARY "X" WITH AN AXE, THAT SHOULD BE ENOUGH FORCE TO CRACK THIS UNSTABLE PACK ICE AND MAKE A CHANNEL BIG ENOUGH FOR US TO SLIP THROUGH.
BRILLIANT!
HOW DO YOU EVEN KNOW THIS RCAN BOAT HAS AN AXE?
BECAUSE, THIS BOAT IS AN AS-4000.
I DESIGNED IT.

AREOPAGITICA
ENJOY THE HOLD, HAFLEY.
LOCK!
WHA--!
POUND POUND POU
STOP BICKERING!
?
FEEL!

I found th MAP!
SHANKS, YOU OLD DOG. YOU DIDN'T HIDE THE MAP -- YOU CARVED IT RIGHT INTO THE WOOD!
FORTUNA-- I NEED YOU!!

WHAT IS IT, HAFLEY?
I WANT SOME, UH, SOME PAPER AND CHARCOAL FOR, UH, DRAWING.
HMM...
OKAY.
REALLY?
SURE.
I'LL GO BUY SOME IN TOWN.
IT'LL GIVE ME AN EXCUSE TO CHECK OUT THE CIRCUS...

"...GOD KNOWS I COULD USE A LAUGH."
A.S.
WHAT'S THAT, ARMY?
JUST SOME SCRIMSHAW I CARRY AROUND WITH ME. A REMINDER OF ANOTHER BROKEN PROMISE.
I STILL THINK WE SHOULD GO STRAIGHT TO BOOTHIA.
BOOTHIA
THIS **SALZAN FLUE** GUY PROBABLY KNOWS AS MUCH ABOUT DNA AS **AMBER**.
WHY ARE YOU IN SUCH A **RUSH** TO GET BACK TO **SCHOOL**?
YOU'VE BEEN PUSHING YOURSELF SO **HARD** THIS SEMESTER...

"LET'S JUST GO TO THE CIRCUS AND **RELAX**."

Lil' Orphan Alley
WELCOME TO YOUR NEW HOME, ALISTAIR.

WHERE'S ANGER THE MAN-BEAST?
DON'T WORRY ABOUT ANGER. HE'S GOT A SHOW TO DO.
BOSS!
RUB
YOU GOT A WARM BODY YET?
GIMME A MINUTE, RONNIE, I'M IN THE MIDDLE OF SOMETHING.
SURE, BOSS. I'LL BE AT THE CAGE.
EVERYONE, LISTEN UP--
I WANT YOU TO MEET YOUR NEW BROTHER-- ALISTAIR CAVENDISH.

LOOKS LIKE YOU'LL FIT RIGHT IN, ALISTAIR.
NOW YOU KIDS PLAY NICE. I'VE GOT A CIRCUS TO RUN.
SO, UH...

...MY BEST FRIEND'S NAME IS ARMY SHANKS!
SHANKS!
SHANKS!
SHANKS!
SHANK
SHAN
DON'T EVER SAY THAT NAME AGAIN!!
OW! OW! WHY ARE YOU PINCHING ME?!?
YOU IDIOT! SHANKS IS THE REASON WE'RE ALL ORPHANS! HE KILLED ALL OUR PARENTS!
AND HE PROBABLY KILLED YOURS TOO!

SOON...
BARK.
BARK.
BARK
BARK.
YES, ALISTAIR...
...BARK LIKE A WILD ANIMAL. GIVE THE PEOPLE WHAT THEY WANT TO SEE!
BARK!
Sob.
BARK
Sob.
BARK

NEARBY...
BARK!!
BARK!!
BARK!!
?
ART
ALISTAIR!
ART
FOX

SOON...
JUST BECAUSE ALISTAIR IS THERE DOESN'T MEAN SHANKS IS AT THE CIRCUS.
THEY PROBABLY HAVEN'T SEEN EACH OTHER IN YEARS.
AREOPAGITICA
?
SHANKS IS AT THE CIRCUS
HA! SHANKS IS LOOKING FOR ME! EAT THAT, PINHO!
WAIT! SHANKS PROBABLY DOESN'T KNOW THAT THE AREOPAGITICA IS HIDDEN SO CLOSE TO HIM!
I'VE GOTTA BREAK OUT OF HERE!

DAMN BARS!
RATTLE!
THINK, HAFLEY...
WHAT WOULD SHANKS DO?
HMM...
WRAP!
WRAP!
BREAK THROUG

SHORTLY...
THERE-- NOW YOU TWO CAN BICKER ALL YOU WANT!
SQUIRM!
SQU
MEANWHILE, I'LL BE HEADING TO THE CIRCUS TO FIND SHANKS!
AND THE TWO OF US ARE GOING TO SAIL AWAY TOGETHER TO FAR ARDEN...
... JUST LIKE WE HAD ORIGINALLY PLANNED!
RCAN
RCAN
AS-4000

LOOK, DAVID, THERE'S THE CIRCUS!
SO WHAT'S THE PLAN, ARMY?
I'VE GOT A GUT FEELING THAT ALISTAIR IS HERE, SO I'M GOING TO LOOK FOR HIM.
BUT I WANT YOU AND DAVID TO BRING THE CODE TO SALZAN FLUE.
THE SOONER WE CAN DECODE THAT MESSAGE...
...THE SOONER WE CAN LEARN WHAT **SIMON ARCTAVIUS** IS TRYING TO TELL US--OR **WARN** US --ABOUT **FAR ARDEN**!

VI

I'M BORED. DO YOU HAVE ANY TOBACCO ON YOU?
THERE'S SOME IN MY COAT POCKET, BUT I CAN'T REACH IT.
PAGITICA
MAN, HOW ABOUT THAT **HAFLEY**! "SHANKS AND I ARE GOING TO SAIL AWAY TOGETHER!"
THAT'S SO **GAY**!
WAIT-- DO YOU HEAR THAT?
WHAT?
SOMETHING ABOUT A POT CALLING A KETTLE BLACK...
I HATE YOU.
TICA

CLIMB!
THERE WE GO...
DUST OFF!
...YOU'RE IN THERE SOMEWHERE, SHANKS.
RUN

Nearby...
HERE.
OH MY!
BUT WHAT'S IT FOR?
BARTY AND RCAN WILL NO DOUBT COME LOOKING FOR US HERE.
WE'LL HIDE IN THE OPEN BY ACTING LIKE A MARRIED COUPLE.
UM... I THINK THAT I SHOULD BE AMBER'S HUSBAND.
BOOTHIA
NO, DAVID. IT'LL MAKE MORE SENSE IF YOU PLAY AMBER'S LITTLE BROTHER.

Mere Paces Away...
SHANKS!
BUT WHAT IS HE DOING WITH THAT GIRL AND HER YOUNGER BROTHER--?
HORRORS!!
YOU NEVER EVEN INTENDED TO COME FIND ME, SHANKS!
RUNAWAY
DID YOU HEAR SOMETHING?
NO, BUT HERE'S WHERE WE SPLIT UP TO LOOK FOR ALISTAIR AND FLUE.
LET'S MEET BACK IN AN HOUR UNDER THAT SIGN THAT SAYS "CAGE MATCH WITH WILD MAN-BEAST / FIGHT TO THE DEATH / NEXT MATCH IN ONE HOUR."
OKAY.
OKAY.

Shortly...
Step Right up for an
EARTH-SHATTER
★ Lecture ★
on the "HOT" topi
GLOBAL WARM
WITH
SALZAN FLU
(author of:)
"THE COLD DELUSION"
"MOUNTING CLIMATE IMPRO
"THE END OF GLACI
and... "LETTER TO AN ARCTIC N

...THE POLAR BEARS ARE OUR CANARIES IN THE MINE SHAFT...

I'M GOING TO GET SOME FRESH AIR. I'LL MEET YOU OUT FRONT WHEN THE LECTURE'S OVER.

HMMM...
LOOK LOOK
BOOTHIA
...THERE WE GO.
So in a Little while...
DAMMIT, DAVID!!
BOOTHIA COLLEGE
SHANKS NEEDS TO COME HERE FOR THIS WHOLE CHARADE TO WORK!
YOU MUST PREVENT THE SCIENTIST SALZAN FLUE FROM DECODING THAT MESSAGE...

...BY **ANY MEANS** **NECESSARY**!
PHONE
I KNOW, I KNOW... AND I **WILL**... IT'S JUST THAT... AMBER... I WANT TO MAKE SURE THAT AMBER DOESN'T GET HURT.
SHE'S JUST A **PAWN** IN THIS WHOLE THING. SHE HAS NO IDEA WHAT SHE'S--
DAVID, **STOP**.
CLEARLY YOU'VE **FALLEN** FOR THIS GIRL. THAT'S NATURAL. BUT WHAT DID I TEACH YOU ON THE **FIRST DAY** OF "BRAIN FUNDAMENTALS"?
THAT... THAT LOVE IS NOTHING MORE THAN A SERIES OF CHEMICAL REACTIONS IN THE BRAIN.
GOOD. NOW GO STOP FLUE. I DON'T WANT TO HEAR FROM YOU AGAIN UNTIL YOU AND SHANKS HAVE MADE IT TO CAMPUS.

HANG UP.
IS EVERYTHING ALRIGHT, PROFESSOR BESSEHL?
OH, OUR MAN IN THE FIELD IS STARTING TO CRACK.
I SUPPOSE I SHOULDN'T HAVE SET HIM UP WITH SUCH A WELL-ENDOWED ACCOMPLI--
KNOCK
KNOC
Quickly! Hide the maps!!
FAR ARDEN?
YANK!
CONCEAL
HIDE!
STUFF!

EMILE?
OH -- YES?
BRAIN
BRAIN
EMILE, I HATE TO DISRUPT YOUR "BRAIN TRUST" CLUB MEETING...
... BUT THE BOYS AND I DOWN IN ACCOUNTING ARE GETTING REAL NERVOUS ABOUT THIS "TOP SECRET PROJECT" OF YOURS.
THE COLLEGE HAS ALREADY SPENT **MILLIONS** OF CANADIAN DOLLARS ON IT AND WE DON'T EVEN KNOW WHAT ***IT*** IS YET!
DON'T WORRY, NEAL...

"...OUR FIRST TEST SUBJECT WILL BE ARRIVING **SOON**..."
ALIST
STEP RIGHT UP AND WATCH **ANGER** THE **MAN-BEAST** -- HALF **MAN** HALF **POLAR BEAR** -- IN THE TOUGHEST FIGHT OF HIS CAREER!
WE CAN'T TELL YOU WHO HIS NEXT VICTIM -- I MEAN **OPPONENT** -- IS...
...BUT TRUST ME WHEN I SAY YOU'RE IN FOR ONE HELLUVA SURPRISE!
!!!

ALISTAIR!!!

HMM...
ANGE
the
MAN
ASSISTANT! COME HERE!
LOUDER, PLEASE.
I SAID THAT I BELIEVE I HAVE FOUND ANGER'S NEXT OPPONENT.
HE'S WEARING A BLUE KNIT CAP AND A MAN-HAULING HARNESS.
BRING HIM IN...
the
MAN·BE
NEXT MATCH · 1 HO

"... USING ANY MEANS NECESSARY!"
... WITH DEVASTATING EFFECTS HERE AND AROUND THE GLOBE.
THANK YOU. THAT CONCLUDES MY LECTURE.
SALZAN FLUE
PFFF! IF IT'S GLOBAL WARMING, HOW COME THERE WAS A COLD SNAP LAST WEEK?
WHAT A FEAR-MONGER!!
... AND IF ANYONE'S INTERESTED, I'LL BE SIGNING COPIES OF MY BOOK OUT FRONT.
SALZAN FLUE
PSST!
?

HELLO? THE BOOK SIGNING WILL BE OUT FRONT--
ACK!
RESTRAIN
CAN YOU READ THIS DNA CODE?
WHAT?
CAN YOU READ WHAT THIS DNA CODE SAYS??
I DON'T KNOW! IT... IT... LOOKS LIKE RNA, NOT DNA -- NOTICE THE URACIL IN PLACE OF THYMINE... ...COULD BE A CODON SEQUENCE, AS IT BEGINS WITH "UAG"...
I'M SORRY, MR. FLUE. I'M GOING TO HAVE TO KILL YOU.

MOPE.
LISTFUL KICK!
"I'LL COME BACK FOR YOU, HAFLEY."
YEAH RIGHT!
sigh...
AREOPAGITICA

"...SO LONG, SHANKS."
C'MON, ALISTAIR, LET'S GET YOU OUT OF THIS CAGE. AMBER AND DAVID ARE--
BARK
WHA--?
ALISTAIR, WHAT'S GOTTEN INTO YOU?
C'MON, PAL, IT'S ME-- YOUR BUDDY SHANKS!

YOU TOLD ME YOU WERE GOING TO HELP ME FIND THE MAN WHO KILLED MY DAD!
... YOU PROMISED!
YEAH, AND I WILL, PAL, BUT RIGHT NOW YOU HAVE TO COME WITH ME...
...AND THEN WE'LL FIND HAFLEY AND THE SHIP... AND SAIL TO FAR ARDEN! ISN'T THAT WHAT YOU WANT?
DID YOU KILL MY DAD?

ALISTAIR...
HEY! BACK OFF, YOU LITTLE SHITS!
TELL ME YOU DIDN'T KILL MY DAD!
I'M SORRY, ALISTAIR...
KNOCK IT OFF! I'M NOT GOING TO FIGHT AGAINST CHILDREN!
ANGRY ORPHAN PUNCH

MEANWHILE...
do-do-doo... JUST WAITIN' OUTSIDE FOR DAVID AND FLUE..
ASTONB
WHAT THE HELL ARE YOU TALKING ABOUT?!?
YOU KNOW TOO MUCH.
YOU HAVE TO DIE.
BOOTHIA
WHIMPER
ALTHOUGH... THERE MAY BE ANOTHER OPTION...
ANYTHING!!

LEAVE. RIGHT NOW.
GO FAR AWAY FROM NUNAVUT AND NEVER LOOK BACK.
NO!
I HAVE TO STAY ON THIS BOOK TOUR!
YOU DON'T UNDERSTAND THE PUBLISHING INDUSTRY -- IT'LL EAT ME ALIVE!!
SO YOU MIGHT AS WELL JUST KILL ME.
UH...

JUST DO IT. I'M NOT REACHING THESE PEOPLE, ANYWAY.
UH...
!
...THE TIRE PILE!
SNAP
HUH?
IF YOU DON'T LEAVE IMMEDIATELY, I'M GOING TO LIGHT THE ASTON BAY TIRE PILE ON FIRE!
OKAY! OKAY! I'M GONE!!
HE, HE. PAT ON THE BACK, DAVID.
PAT PAT
SCREAM!!
!

HUMAN-SIZED BITE!!
!

NO!
BOOTHIA

NO ONE WAS ACTUALLY SUPPOSED TO **DIE**...!

CRACKLE!
WHO'S READY TO SEE A BEAST DEVOUR A MAN!!!
WHA...
THIS CAN'T BE GOOD.
FIGHT to the DEATH!
ANGER VS. Shanks

BICKER!
BICKER!
BICKER
SLICE
HAFLEY, WHAT ARE YOU DOING?!
I FOUND THE MAP, PINHO.
WE'RE GOING TO FAR ARDEN.

VII

YOU WERE RIGHT, PINHO. SHANKS NEVER MEANT TO COME BACK FOR ME.
HE'S AT THE CIRCUS WITH SOME **GIRL**.
WHAT?!
FORTUNA, WHERE THE DEVIL ARE YOU GOING? WE'RE SETTING SAIL FOR--
YOU TWO CAN **HAVE** FAR ARDEN. ALL I EVER WANTED WAS ARMY.
GOODBYE, PINHO.
WELL, HAFLEY...

"...LOOKS LIKE IT'S JUST YOU AND ME NOW!"
TH!
Shanks
PREPARE YOURSELVES for the ULTIMATE battle of MAN vs. BEAST...
...CUNNING vs. BRUTE FORCE...
...and REASON...

"...vs. PASSION!"
ARMY!!!
ARMY!

Nearby...
DAVID!
ARMY!
ARM
AR--
AR--
!
SO IT'S TRUE!!
RUN AWAY!

PUSH OFF!!
DOOF!
MID-AIR GROIN GRINDER
TUCK 'n' ROLL...
...and RECOVER!

GROAN
MISS!!
DODGE!
YOU DON'T WANT TO FIGHT ME, ANGER!
I JUST GOT BEAT UP BY A BUNCH OF ORPHANS AND I'M NOT TOO HAPPY!!
MISS
WHAT ARE YOU DOING HERE, ANYWAY?
A TALENTED, HANDSOME GUY LIKE YOU COULD DO A LOT BETTER THAN A TRAVELING CIRCUS!
DUCK!

UH... ANY SECOND NOW, ANGER'LL MAKE MINCE MEAT OUT OF HIS DOOMED OPPONENT!
THIS FIGHT SUCKS!
YEAH! IF I WANTED TO HEAR SOMEONE TALK I WOULD'VE GONE TO THAT GLOBAL WARMING LECTURE.
YEAH!
HIGH-FIVE!
YOU'RE TOO BIG FOR THIS RACKET, ANGER. YOU SHOULD--
R LL!
NO! I AM LOYAL TO THE CIRCUS! HERE I HAVE A HOME... A FAMILY...
...HERE I AM A STAR!
SCOOP!

Meanwhile, right outside...
the MAN-BEAST
NEXT MATCH -- 1 HR
ARMY
HMM...
PEEK
GASP!
ARMY!
UH...
UH...
INHALE!

FIRE!
FIGHT DEATH!
ANGER
!
KS
No! STOP RUNNING AROUND IN PANIC! SIT DOWN IN YOUR CHAIRS AND ENJOY THE FIGHT!

THIS IS IT, ANGER. YOUR BIG CHANCE TO ESCAPE.
LOOK AROUND.
YOU'RE NOT A STAR HERE...
...YOU'RE A PRISONER.
CAST ASIDE
NNGG!

Elsewhere...
...IT WASN'T YOUR FAULT, DAVE ... THAT POLAR BEAR WOULD'VE EATEN HIM EVEN IF YOU HADN'T MADE HIM RUN OUTSIDE...
...THAT'S JUST WHAT POLAR BEARS DO... THEY EAT PEOPLE...
BOOTHIA
...ESPECIALLY NOWADAYS, WITH UH... DEPLETED FOOD SOURCES, BECAUSE OF, UH ... GLOBAL WARMING.
...YEAH, IT'S GLOBAL WARMING'S FAULT!
COMMOTION COMMOTION!!
?
BOOTHIA

ANGER, NO!
GET BACK IN YOUR CAGE!
I'M WARNING YOU, ANGER!
HEY! DON'T WALK AWAY FROM ME!!
ANGER! ANGER... UH...
HELLO, FRIEND.

SOON...
SNUB
ARMY!
ARMY! I'M SO GLAD YOU'RE ALRIGHT!
DID YOU FIND ALISTAIR? HAVE YOU SEEN DAVID?
LET'S GO TALK TO FLUE! MAYBE DAVID IS BACK-STAGE WITH HIM OR SOMETHING.
NO.
HUG
IT'S NOT SAFE HERE ANYMORE. I WANT TO HEAD TO BOOTHIA COLLEGE AS SOON AS POSSIBLE.

Around the corner...
psst.
OH, HI, ALISTAIR.
HI.
LISTEN, UH...
BOATHIA
...SOMETHING BAD HAPPENED AND I NEED TO SORT SOME THINGS OUT. **LIFE** THINGS. SO I CAN'T HANG OUT WITH YOU AND SHANKS ANYMORE.
ARMY ISN'T MY FRIEND. I HATE HIM.
OH.
THAT'S A ONE-EIGHTY.

Shortly...
DAVID! ALISTAIR! YAY! THE TEAM'S BACK TOGETHER!!
OH, ALISTAIR!
WE MISSED YOU SO MUCH!
AND DAVID! I WANT TO GIVE YOU A BIG BEAR HUG!

KNOCK IT OFF!
HUG
HA HA
NOW C'MON -- WE'VE GOT TO GET GOING!
NO.
WE'RE GOING TO SKIP FLUE AND JUST HEAD STRAIGHT TO BOOTHIA COLLEGE TO SEE YOUR PROFESSOR...
AMBER.
YOU WERE RIGHT, DAVID. WE SHOULD HAVE JUST HEADED THERE IN THE FIRST--
AMBER.
WE'RE NOT GOING WITH YOU.
BOOTHI
ASTO NBAY

PULL ASIDE
DAVID? WHAT'S GOTTEN INTO YOU?
SHANKS IS **TROUBLE**, AMBER. LET HIM GO TO BOOTHIA BY HIMSELF.
DAVID, THAT'S CRAZY! SHANKS ISN'T **TROUBLE**, HE JUST WANTS TO READ THAT LETTER FROM HIS FRIEND!
AMBER, THAT LETTER ISN'T...
WHAT?
...IT ISN'T THAT SIMPLE.

FORGET ABOUT SHANKS AND THE LETTER, DAVID.
WE'RE STICKING TOGETHER BECAUSE YOU AND I ARE A **TEAM** AND WE **LOVE** EACH OTHER!
FACE AWAY
DAVID...? DAVID, TELL ME YOU LOVE ME.
BOOTHIA
SO THAT'S IT, THEN.
ALISTAIR, COME ON.

UNBELIEVABLE.

DID I JUST HALLUCINATE? AM I TAKING CRAZY PILLS?
HOW DO MY EYES LOOK? ARE THEY DILATED?
YER FINE.
I KNOW I SHOULD BE BLUBBERING LIKE AN IDIOT RIGHT NOW, BUT I'M TOO SHOCKED TO FEEL ANYTHING AT ALL.
... IT'S AS IF OUR ENTIRE RELATIONSHIP MEANT ABSOLUTELY NOTHING...
WAIT!...
...BEFORE WE "BORROW" THIS SHIP...
...LET'S MAKE SURE THERE'S SOME FOOD ON BOARD.
Minsky

SO WHERE ARE WE GOING?
I DON'T KNOW. ANYWHERE BUT HERE.
BOOTHIA
HOW 'BOUT THAT BIG **TIRE PILE**?
NO.
HOW 'BOUT THE **OCEAN**?
NO.
THEN HOW 'BOUT THAT **MOUNTAIN VALLEY**?

THE WHOLE POINT OF FINDING FAR ARDEN WAS TO FULFILL A PROMISE TO A FRIEND...
...SO THERE'D BE ONE LESS PERSON IN THE WORLD MAD AT ME.
INSTEAD, IT'S DESTROYING EVERY RELATIONSHIP AROUND ME.
WELL...

...NOT EVERY ONE.

VIII

MEANWHILE...
ROYAL CANADIAN ARCTIC NAVY

ALRIGHT, LET'S GO OVER IT AGAIN...
I ALREADY TOLD YOU...
THE PIRATE, SHANKS, SNUCK INTO MY FAMILY-FRIENDLY ESTABLISHMENT...
...DESTROYED MY MAIN ACT...
...AND KILLED MY KEYNOTE SPEAKER!

SHANKS DIDN'T KILL FLUE.
EXCUSE ME? WHO ARE YOU TWO?
COPS OF A SPECIAL "NATURE"...
FLUE WAS KILLED BY A POLAR BEAR OUT-SIDE OF HIS TENT.
...ENVIRONMENTAL COPS!
IT'S NO SECRET THAT MELTING POLAR ICE IS FORCING BEARS TO GO INLAND TO SEARCH FOR FOOD.
THEN TRULY IT WAS NOT A MAN (SMALL m) BUT MAN (CAPITAL M) THAT KILLED THE NOTED ENVIRONMENTAL SCIENTIST SALZAN FLUE.
WELL PUT.
THANK YOU.

GREAT. THEN GO FIND THE POLAR BEAR AND EX-TINGUISH IT. ONCE BEARS HAVE THE TASTE OF MAN...
TOO LATE FOR THAT. THE BEAR'S TRACKS LEAD STRAIGHT INTO THE VALLEY.
HE'S PROBABLY MILES AWAY BY NOW.
I DON'T CARE ABOUT THE BEAR!
DO YOU KNOW WHERE SHANKS IS HEADED?
LET ME THINK...
YOU KNOW, I DID HEAR SOMEONE MENTION BOOTHIA COLLEGE--
BESSEHL!!!

ARMY! WHY ARE YOU PULLING DOWN THE SAIL!?
THE WIND QUIT ON US.
GOOD TIME TO REST UNTIL THE BREEZE PICKS UP AGAIN.
IN ANY CASE, THE CURRENT SHOULD TAKE US RIGHT TO BOOTHIA.
HERE...

...TRY SOME OF THIS.
A PUB NEAR MY HOUSE TRIED TO DISTILL ITS OWN WHISKEY A FEW YEARS AGO.
THE WHOLE ENTERPRISE WAS A COMPLETE DISASTER, BUT AT LEAST I GOT A FEW FREE BOTTLES OUT OF IT.
HOW IS IT?
IT'S GOOD.
SAY, UH... AT THE CIRCUS I SAW A BLONDE WOMAN LOOKING FOR YOU.
AST
BAY
OH.

YOU KNOW, ARMY, I'VE DECIDED--
HMM?
I'VE DECIDED TO **QUIT SCHOOL** AND FOLLOW YOU TO **FAR ARDEN**!
UH-HUH.
I MEAN, I IMAGINE THAT FAR ARDEN IS A PRETTY **BIG** ISLAND...
...SO I WOULDN'T GET IN YOUR WAY...

"...UNLESS YOU WANTED ME TO."
AREOPAGI
I REALLY DON'T THINK THAT'S A GOOD IDEA, PINHO.
TAKING THE FIGUREHEAD OFF A SHIP IS REALLY BAD LUCK.
AREOPAGITICA
NO DICE, HAFLEY. I DON'T WANT ANY REMINDERS OF FORTUNA ON THIS SHIP...
...ESPECIALLY SHANKS' CRUDE EFFIGY OF HER AS A SIREN.

In a Little While...
THERE.
NOW, HAFLEY, SINCE YOU'RE SO WORRIED ABOUT **DISASTER** ...
... I THINK THIS IS A GOOD TIME FOR YOU TO TELL ME WHERE THE **MAP** IS. YOU KNOW, IN CASE SOMETHING **HAPPENS** TO ONE OF US.
SORRY, PINHO. THAT MAP IS MY ONLY **LEVERAGE**.
YES, WELL, PERHAPS YOUR **LIPS** WILL BE A LITTLE **LOOSER** AT DINNER TONIGHT...
Greenland®
HIGH ALCOHOL CONTENT

"...AFTER I WEAR YOU DOWN!"
I DON'T LIKE LONG WALKS ANYMORE.
I CAN'T EVEN SEE THE CIRCUS ANYMORE.
AND I'M HUNGRY!

ALRIGHT, ALRIGHT.
UH...
...THERE! I SEE A LAKE.
WHAT'RE YOU GONNA DO?
I'M GOING TO CATCH A FISH!
IF SHANKS CAN DO IT, HOW HARD CAN IT BE?
BOOT
DIVE!

But Soon...
SO... COLD...
IT'S ALRIGHT. I'VE ALMOST STARVED TO DEATH **HUNDREDS** OF TIMES.
SHIVE
SHIV
SH
SCREAM!!!
?
RUN
DAVID, IT'S THE **BLONDE** LADY.
SHE'S BEING ATTACKED BY A **POLAR BEAR**!

HELP!
ROAR!!!
NO! I CAN'T WATCH ANOTHER PERSON GET **EATEN**--
ROAR
THROW UP A LITTL
IN MOUTH
ALISTAIR, BARK LIKE A FOX OR SOMETHING! **DISTRACT** IT!
NO! SHE'S A FRIEND OF MY DAD'S **KILLER**. SHE DOESN'T DESERVE MY HELP.
HEY, SOMEONE'S COMING!

BOOF!!
MID-AIR GROIN GRINDER

ANGER!
BOOTHIA
PUNCH!
THROW
ANGER!
ALISTAIR?
ALISTAIR, MY YOUNG FRIEND!
HUG!

AFTER OUR ENJOYABLE BOAT RIDE I DIDN'T THINK I'D EVER SEE YOU AGAIN!
THE CIRCUS WARDEN PUT ME IN A CAGE AND CALLED ME "FOX CUB BOY" AND MADE ME **BARK** FOR PEOPLE!
I KNOW, HE TURNED OUT TO BE A PRETTY BAD MAN.
ARE YOU OKAY?
WAIT, ARE YOU GOING SOMEWHERE, ANGER?
YES! I'M TRAVELING TO VANCOUVER (CANADA'S HOLLYWOOD) TO BE A **MOVIE STAR**!
AND I HAVE YOUR FRIEND SHANKS TO THANK!
I HIGHLY DOUBT **THAT**.
KICK

CHOMP
!
!
!
ANGER!
ARGH!!
SAVE YOURSELF, ALISTAIR!
GO!!

LATER...
BOOTHIA

RCAN
DOES EVERYONE WEAR RCAN SHIRTS AROUND HERE?
IT'S MY HUSBAND'S. HE USED TO BE AN OFFICER.
RUMMAG
RCAN

WHERE'S YOUR HUSBAND NOW?
OH. WE HAD A...
...A FALLING OUT.
TWIST OFF
SO I DECIDED TO BE A HERMIT FOR A WHILE AND LIVE OFF THE LAND.
I SECOND THAT. AFTER TODAY I JUST WANT TO CRAWL IN A HOLE AND NEVER COME OUT.
AND I THIRD THAT! I CAN'T BELIEVE I WAS FRIENDS WITH SHANKS -- THE MAN WHO KILLED MY FATHER!
OH, YOU POOR THING.
YOU DON'T KNOW, DO YOU?
RCAN

SHANKS IS YOUR FATHER
RCAN

'S BROTHER!
ARMY'S MY UNCLE?
THAT'S RIGHT.
THEN... THEN ARMY MURDERED HIS OWN BROTHER!
THAT'S FRATRICIDE.
NO, NO, NO... LET ME EXPLAIN WHAT HAPPENED...

SHANKS HAD AN OLDER BROTHER NAMED **ELIOT**.
ELIOT IS YOUR BIOLOGICAL DAD, AND HE LOVED YOU VERY MUCH.
BUT THEN A STRANGER KILLED ELIOT (FOR REASONS I WON'T GO INTO)...
POTATO SACK
STRAN
...AND YOUR MOTHER DIS-APPEARED, SO YOU WENT INTO FOSTER CARE.
foster dad →
ARMY WAS ON A LONG SEA JOURNEY, BUT HE CAME HOME WHEN HE HEARD HIS BROTHER DIED.
!
NO ONE KNEW WHO HAD KILLED ELIOT, SO ARMY SEARCHED AND SEARCHED...
POTATO SACK

...AND EVENTUALLY DISCOVERED THAT IT WAS YOUR **FOSTER DAD** WHO HAD KILLED YOUR FATHER!
ARMY KILLED YOUR FOSTER DAD AS REVENGE.
SO IN A WAY, ARMY **DID** KILL YOUR DAD. JUST NOT YOUR BIOLOGICAL ONE.
OH.
EVERYONE TREATED SHANKS LIKE A HERO. BUT AFTER THE MURDER, HE RETREATED INSIDE HIMSELF...
...AND REFUSED TO LET ANYONE IN.

IX

YOU KNOW, FORTUNA, YOU HARDLY MENTIONED ALISTAIR'S **MOTHER**. WHERE WERE **YOU** DURING ALL THIS?
DID YOU KNOW MY MOTHER? WHAT WAS SHE LIKE??
I WAS DATING SHANKS AT THE TIME, DAVID.
ALISTAIR, I **DID** KNOW YOUR MOTHER. SHE... SHE WAS A TRAIN WRECK.
SHE WAS SO NEGLECTFUL THAT SHE NAMED YOU AFTER HER FAVORITE TOBACCO, JUST SO SHE WOULDN'T FORGET YOUR NAME.
OH.
EVENTUALLY, AFTER YOUR FATHER'S DEATH...

"... SHE JUST DISAPPEARED."
WHEN ARE WE **LEAVING**, PINHO?
RELAX, HAFLEY, AND EAT.
AREOPAGITICA
WE CAN'T START A TREACHEROUS VOYAGE WITHOUT A CIVILIZED MEAL, NOW CAN WE?
POUR
BESIDES, I SPENT ALL EVENING ON THIS FEAST.
THERE YOU GO. DRINK UP.
AND WHILE WE'RE EATING...
...I'LL TELL YOU EVERYTHING I KNOW ABOUT **FAR ARDEN**!

SHANKS AND I WERE STUDENTS AT THE ARCTIC ACADEMY.
WE HAD A HISTORY CLASS TOGETHER, TAUGHT BY A MAN NAMED SIMON ARCTAVIUS.
AA
I DIDN'T KNOW MUCH ABOUT SHANKS AT THE TIME...
AA
AA
...ONLY THAT HE WAS A TEACHER'S PET BECAUSE OF HIS SAILING PROWESS.
?

ONE DAY ARCTAVIUS WAS TEACHING US ABOUT ARCTIC MYTHS AND LEGENDS.
IT WAS ALL PRETTY LIGHT-HEARTED STUFF...
Symmes' Hole
...UNTIL HE STARTED TALKING ABOUT FAR ARDEN, AND THEN ALL OF A SUDDEN HE GOT EXTREMELY SERIOUS AND PASSIONATE.
HE WENT ON A LONG TANGENT ABOUT HOW THIS MYSTERIOUS ISLAND -- A TROPICAL PARADISE IN THE MIDDLE OF THE BARREN CANADIAN ARCTIC --
--MIGHT ACTUALLY BE REAL!
FAR
ARDEN

HE TALKED ABOUT HOW AN ENTIRE TRIBE OF **NORSEMEN** FROM GREENLAND SUPPOSEDLY ALL PICKED UP AND LEFT FOR FAR ARDEN, AND WERE NEVER HEARD FROM AGAIN.

HE EXPLAINED HOW OCEAN CURRENTS BEHAVE **ERRATICALLY** IN A CERTAIN PART OF THE ARCTIC OCEAN, IN WAYS THAT CAN'T BE EXPLAINED SCIENTIFICALLY.

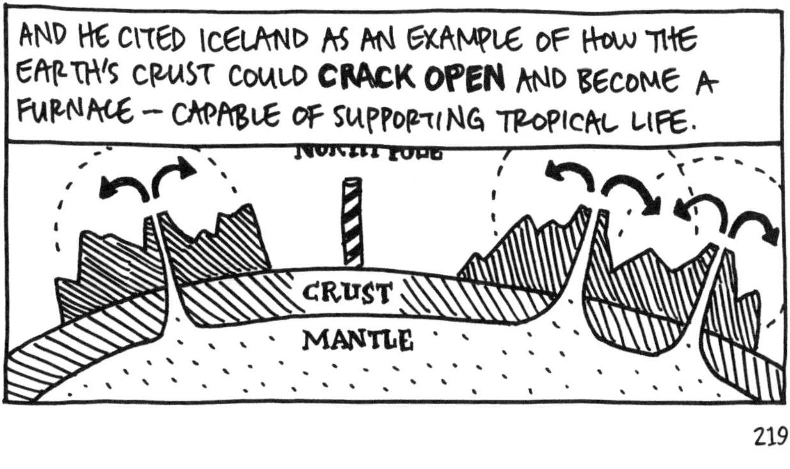
AND HE CITED ICELAND AS AN EXAMPLE OF HOW THE EARTH'S CRUST COULD **CRACK OPEN** AND BECOME A FURNACE — CAPABLE OF SUPPORTING TROPICAL LIFE.
CRUST
MANTLE

EVERYONE IN THE CLASS LAUGHED AT ARCTAVIUS, EXCEPT FOR FOUR OF US.
HA
HA
HA
HA
HA
WE THEN WATCHED HIM COMPOSE HIMSELF, AND SAY THAT FAR ARDEN WAS NOTHING MORE THAN A MYTH. A STORY.
BUT THE FOUR OF US HAD SEEN THE PASSION IN HIS EYES.
WE KNEW RIGHT THEN THAT THERE WAS **TRUTH** TO FAR ARDEN, A TRUTH THE ACADEMY WAS MAKING HIM SUPPRESS.
FAR ARDEN?

I CAN'T BELIEVE THAT ARMY KNEW THE TRUTH ABOUT ME THIS WHOLE TIME!
WHY DIDN'T HE **SAY** ANYTHING?
<HIC>
YOU'RE NOT THE ONLY ONE WHO WANTS TO PICK SHANKS' **BRAIN**!
I'VE GOT A STORY ABOUT YOUR UNCLE THAT WILL BLOW YOUR...
... "**MIND**"?
EH?
UH, I THINK YOU MAYBE OVERDID IT ON THE WINE.
DRINK
I FINE. I FINE.

SO ANYWAY, ... THIS STORY'S ABOUT A PROFESSOR ... WHO WANTS SOMETHING FROM SHANKS.
SO HE DECIDES TO STEAL IT.
RCAN
ONLY THING IS... WHAT HE WANTS... IS IN SHANKS' BRAIN!
SO I SAY, "HEY PROFESSOR, I'M A NICE GUY, I'LL HELP YOU BRING IN THIS SHANKS GUY."
AND HE SAYS, "DAVID, IT'S NOT THAT SIMPLE. WHAT I'M TRYING TO DO IS, I'M TRYING TO READ HIS MIND..."
"... SO YOU CAN'T JUST DRAG HIM IN. HE'S GOTTA BE IN THE RIGHT FRAME OF MIND."

SO MY PROFESSOR, HE PLANS A RUSE.
WHAT'S A RUSE?
EH, IT'S A TRICK, A DECEPTION...
...A LIE.
SO HE SITS ME DOWN AND HE SAYS...
DAVID, THIS IS COMPLICATED, SO PAY ATTENTION.
BOOTHIA

"THERE IS A GIRL ON CAMPUS WHO IS EXACTLY SHANKS' TYPE-- STUBBORN, INTELLIGENT, AND BUXOM.
"I WANT YOU TO START DATING HER.
"SLOWLY, BEGIN TELLING HER STORIES ABOUT AN HEROIC AND HANDSOME ARCTIC PIRATE NAMED SHANKS.
"WHEN SHE IS SUFFICIENTLY SEDUCED BY THIS MYTH, LET ME KNOW...
"...AND I'LL ARRANGE IT SO THIS GIRL WILL ENCOUNTER AN OLD FISHERMAN WHO WILL SAY THAT HE RECENTLY FOUND A LETTER ADDRESSED TO SHANKS, AND WOULD SHE DELIVER IT?

"SHE'LL MAKE UP AN EXCUSE TO GO VISIT SHANKS..."
BOOTHIA Tattler
...AND YOU, DAVID, WILL TAG ALONG AND MAKE SURE THAT SHANKS DECIDES TO COME HERE -- BOOTHIA COLLEGE -- WHERE I'LL BE WAITING FOR HIM!!
AND HERE WE ARE. EVERYTHING WENT ACCORDING TO PLAN, JUST LIKE HE SAID IT WOULD.
LONG LIVE PROFESSOR BESSEHL!
NO! ... NOT BESSEHL!!
RCAN
YOU DON'T KNOW BESSEHL. HE'S A SOCIOPATH!
SHANKS IS WALKING INTO A TRAP...
RCA

"...AND WE'VE GOT TO **STOP** HIM!"
SO THE FOUR OF US AND ARCTAVIUS STARTED AN AFTER-SCHOOL GROUP CALLED **THE SCRIMSHAW CLUB.**
ARCTAVIUS PRETENDED TO BE TEACHING US HOW TO CARVE ON BONE...
...BUT REALLY WE WERE DISCUSSING AND RESEARCHING FAR ARDEN.
IF SOMEONE WALKED IN ON US WE WOULD PRETEND TO CARVE UNTIL THEY WENT AWAY.

LIKE I SAID, THERE WERE FOUR OF US.
SHANKS WAS QUIET. A HISTORY BUFF AND THE BEST SAILOR IN THE ACADEMY.
ME, MY PASSION WASN'T SAILING SO MUCH AS THE NAVY ITSELF.
THIRD WAS BARTY REDGRAVE. HE WASN'T VERY BOOKSMART BUT COULD CHARM THE NOSE OFF AN ELEPHANT SEAL.
AA
FINALLY, THERE WAS EMILE BESSEHL. HE WAS THE DRIVING FORCE BEHIND THE CLUB.
AA
AA
BESSEHL'S ONE PASSION WAS EXPLORATION, AND HIS HEART LEAPT TO DISCOVER THAT THERE WAS ONE MORE BLANK SPOT ON THE MAP...

"... ONE MORE DARK CORNER OF THE EARTH TO DISCOVER."
SHANKS IS THE ONLY PERSON WHO SAW ARCTAVIUS' MAP TO FAR ARDEN.
BESSEHL MUST THINK THE MAP IS STILL BACK THERE, HIDING IN THE DEEP RECESSES OF HIS **MEMORY**.
AND BESSEHL'S GOING TO **EXTRACT** IT SOMEHOW..
... AND I LET AMBER GO WITH HIM!
WHAT DO WE **DO**?
UNCLIP
RCA
THE ONLY THING WE **CAN** DO...

"...WE'RE GOING TO COMMANDEER THE AREOPAGITICA."
POUR
THE WINE-- IS IT GOOD?
DRINK UP, DRINK UP.
AREOPAGITICA
SO ANYWAY, HAFLEY, THE SCRIMSHAW CLUB MET ONCE A WEEK FOR YEARS...
...POURING OVER OLD LEGENDS AND TEASING OUT POSSIBLE CLUES TO FAR ARDEN'S WHEREABOUTS.
THE MORE EVIDENCE WE FOUND, THE MORE COMMITTED WE WERE TO FINDING THE ISLAND AND SPENDING OUR DAYS IN LUXURY.

THE SECRET MEETINGS CONTINUED, EVEN AS WE GRADUATED FROM THE ACADEMY...
...AND ALL ENLISTED IN RCAN.
I ADMIT, THERE WERE TIMES WHEN OUR ENTHUSIASM WANED, ESPECIALLY WHEN GIRLS WERE CONCERNED.
WE NEVER ABANDONED THE SEARCH FOR THE ISLAND, BUT FOR A FEW YEARS THE MEETINGS BECAME MONTHLY, OR EVEN MORE INFREQUENT.
BUT THAT CHANGED ONCE WE HEARD THAT A DERANGED MAN HAD STUMBLED INTO A BAR IN DEVON...
...CLAIMING TO HAVE BEEN TO FAR ARDEN!!

MOST PEOPLE DIDN'T BELIEVE THIS MAN, WHO WAS OBVIOUSLY TRAUMATIZED BY THE LOSS OF HIS SON.
BUT ARCTAVIUS KEPT AN OPEN MIND. HE INTERVIEWED THE MAN...
WRITE
WRIT
...AND BY MATCHING THE MAN'S ACCOUNT TO OUR YEARS OF DATA...
...ARCTAVIUS WAS ABLE TO DEVISE A PLAUSIBLE MAP TO FAR ARDEN!
SO THE FIVE OF US MADE PLANS FOR A VOYAGE, WITH THE MAP LOCKED AWAY IN ARCTAVIUS' MIND.

BUT THEN THE BUREAUCRATS TOOK OVER RCAN, AND SHANKS AND ARCTAVIUS STUPIDLY FORMED A RESISTANCE.
THEY WERE EXILED TO EGLINTON ISLAND, PRESUMABLY TO THEIR DEATHS.
RCA
ASSUMING THEY WERE DEAD AND GONE, THE REST OF US WENT ON WITH OUR LIVES.
I STAYED IN RCAN AND BECAME AN OFFICER...
...BARTY WENT INTO POLITICS...
SHAKE!
...AND BESSEHL WENT TO A PRIVATE COLLEGE TO STUDY **BIOLOGY**...
TAP TAP

"...I GUESS HE WANTED A CHANGE OF PACE!"
HURRY! THE SHIP MIGHT STILL BE THERE!
RUN
RUN
RUN
WHY DID I LET AMBER GO WITH SHANKS??
I'M SO STUPID!
SHH! I SEE IT!
FROM THIS POINT ON, NOBODY MAKE A SOUND!...

"... WE HAVE TO SURPRISE THEM!"
TO EVERYONE'S AMAZEMENT, SHANKS AND ARCTAVIUS SURVIVED.
AREOPAGITICA
IT WAS CLEAR THAT THEY HAD FORMED SOME SORT OF BOND...
BARBER
... AND ACTIVELY KEPT ME AND BARTY AND BESSEHL OUT OF THE LOOP.
A YEAR LATER ARCTAVIUS SAILED TO FAR ARDEN, HAVING SHARED THE MAP ONLY WITH SHANKS.
HANDSHAKE!!
SHANKS WAS SUPPOSED TO FOLLOW HIM IN THE AREOPAGITICA, BUT NEVER DID.

ARCTAVIUS NEVER RETURNED, WHICH FOR **SOME** PEOPLE WOULD BE A BAD SIGN.
BUT HE WAS THE BEST SAILOR IN THE ARCTIC. FOR HIM NOT TO RETURN SURELY MEANT THAT HE **FOUND** IT.
SO FOR THE LAST THREE YEARS, FORTUNA AND I HAVE LIVED UNDERGROUND, DEDICATING OUR LIVES TO FINDING FAR ARDEN.

DURING FORTUNA'S BRIEF RELATIONSHIP WITH SHANKS, SHE HAD LEARNED THAT SHANKS HAD HIDDEN THE MAP TO FAR ARDEN ABOARD THIS SHIP.
ARCTAVIUS HAD ALWAYS KEPT THE MAP IN HIS HEAD, BUT SHANKS ADMITTED THAT IT WAS TOO COMPLICATED FOR HIM, SO HE NEEDED TO WRITE IT DOWN.
UNFORTUNATELY, SOMEONE STOLE THE SHIP, AND FORTUNA AND I THOUGHT THAT THE MAP WAS LOST FOREVER!
ARE OF
CLIMB!
CLIMB!

BUT WE KEPT SEARCHING... AND SEARCHING... AND FINALLY HAD A BIG BREAK RECENTLY WHEN WE FOUND THE SHIP DRY-DOCKED IN A SALVAGE YARD IN DISKO.
AREOPAGITICA
SO WE PUT AN AD IN SHANKS' NEWSPAPER, ADVERTISING THAT THE AREOPAGITICA WAS FOR SALE.
SHIP FOR SALE
★ CHEAP! ★
KNOWN AS
AREOPAGITICA
"STRANGE NAME, GREAT PRICE"
THREE MAST BRIG
SALVAGE DEAL
UNKNOWN OWNER
EGLINTON PINE KEEL
LOOKS HAND MADE
THE AD SAID TO MEET THE ANONYMOUS SELLER AT THE SOMBER MOOSE AT A SPECIFIC TIME ON A SPECIFIC DAY.
SHANKS, IT'S HERE! DOCKED RIGHT OUT FRONT...

AND YOU KNOW THE REST, HAFLEY.
hic.
THE TRICK WAS TO GET SHANKS ON BOARD...
OPEN
...AND FORCE HIM INTO SHOWING US WHERE HE HID THE MAP.
BUT NOW YOU FOUND IT, HAFLEY!
RECORK
SO NOW... IF YOU WOULDN'T MIND DIVULGING THAT NUGGET OF INFORMATION--
WAIT.
DID YOU HEAR SOMETHING?

X

THE NEXT MORNING...
FLAP
FLAP
FLAP

FLAP
FLAP
WHY ARE YOU CRYING?
I MISS DAVID.
WHAT HAPPENED TO QUITTING SCHOOL AND GOING TO FAR ARDEN?
I CAN'T MAKE UP MY MIND!

MEANWHILE...
FLAP
FLAP
FLAP
AWAKEN
BOO
TIE
SORRY, I MUST HAVE DOZED OFF OR SOMETHING--
BOOTHIA
THAT'S FINE, WE HAVEN'T HAD ANY WIND UNTIL NOW. WOULD YOU GRAB THE MIZZEN LINE?
BOOTHIA

UHH...
LISTEN, FORTUNA--
LOOK WHAT I FOUND!
YAR! I CAN SEE YER PRIVATES!!
GOOD. WE CAN PUT ALISTAIR IN A CROW'S NEST AND HAVE HIM BE A LOOKOUT.
NO... HE'S PROBABLY AFRAID OF HEIGHTS LIKE HIS FATHER...
UH, FORTUNA?

HUH?
BOOTHIA
I JUST WANTED TO SAY HOW SORRY I AM FOR GETTING SHANKS INVOLVED IN ALL THIS...
...I HONESTLY HAD NO IDEA THAT I WAS PUTTING HIM -- OR AMBER -- IN DANGER...
DAVID, STOP.
IT HAPPENED. APOLOGIES ARE WORTHLESS NOW.
IF YOU'RE **TRULY** SORRY, YOU'LL SHOW THAT THROUGH YOUR **ACTIONS**.
AND BASED ON YOUR HELP OBTAINING THIS SHIP LAST NIGHT...

"...I BELIEVE YOU GENUINELY **DO** WANT TO HELP SHANKS AND AMBER."
SO THIS IS BOOTHIA COLLEGE.
BOOTHIA COLLEGE
Ming
WHY DON'T I SEE ANY KIDS AROUND?
IT'S SPRING BREAK. ONLY THE NERDS STAY ON CAMPUS.

DO YOU THINK DAVID'S PROFESSOR WILL BE HERE?
PROBABLY.
DAVID SAYS HE'S WORKING ON SOME BIG RESEARCH PROJECT, SO HE PROBABLY LOVES THE PEACE AND QUIET.
ANYWAY, I'LL RUN IN AND HAVE HIM DECODE ARCTAVIUS' MESSAGE!
YEP.
I'LL JUST WAIT HERE UNTIL I GET BORED!

BIOLOGY DEPT.
RUN
HEY, YOU'RE DAVID'S FRIENDS, RIGHT?
THIS IS GOING TO SOUND TOTALLY RANDOM, BUT DO YOU KNOW WHERE I CAN FIND HIS NEUROSCIENCE PROFESSOR?
YES.
WE'LL TAKE YOU THERE.
THANKS!!

MEANWHILE, BACK IN ASTON BAY...
HURRY UP, HAFLEY!
I'M TOO TIRED...
TIRED? FROM WHAT? YOU HARDLY PUT UP ANY FIGHT AT ALL LAST NIGHT!
MAYBE I COULD HAVE IF YOU HADN'T GOTTEN ME SO GODDAMN DRUNK!!

BICKER
BICKER
YOO-HOO ♫
WHICH ONE OF YOU BOYS WANTS A MASSAGE?
NO THANK YOU, MA'AM!!
SCAMPER!!
BEARDED LADY

Huff 'n' Puff
HUH?
...IF THERE'S ONE THING I LEARNED FROM RCAN, IT'S TO ALWAYS GET A GOOD NIGHT'S SLEEP BEFORE A BIG--
BARTY!!
?
PINHO?
WHAT ARE YOU DOING HERE?

AREOPAGITICA
WE'RE MAKING GOOD TIME.
I HAVE TO SAY, ARMY AND SIMON DID A HELLUVA JOB BUILDING THIS SHIP.
A
HEY...
...WHAT'S **THAT?**

RCAN
I SEE THEM, SIR...
...IT'S DEFINITELY THE AREOPAGITICA.
RCAN
AND YOU THINK SHANKS IS ON THAT SHIP, PINHO?
NO...

"...BUT THAT SHIP WILL LEAD US RIGHT TO HIM."
MINSKY
BORED SIGH
BORED KICK
AMBER.
BOOTH
COLLE
AMBER? HELLO?
BIOLOGY DEPT.

AMBER?
TREE
AME
e Future of Neuroscience:
AugCog
UGMENTED COGNITION)
--WHA...?
DIR. OF AUGCOG STUDIES
PROF. EMILE BESSEHL
BESSEHL!!

LIGHTS FLICKER!
WHAT THE--
SPIN
HEY!!
WRA

DAMMIT!
RUN
HIT
BREAK!
BOUN
THAT'S MY PIPE! YOU ASSHOLE!
KICK!

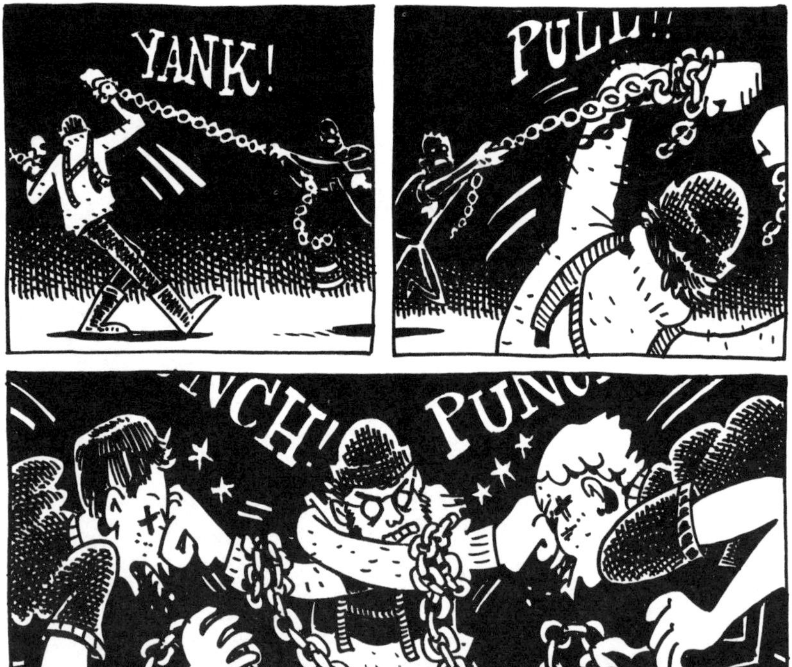
YANK!
PULL!!
NCH!
PUN
CAST ASIDE
GROAN...
GROAN...

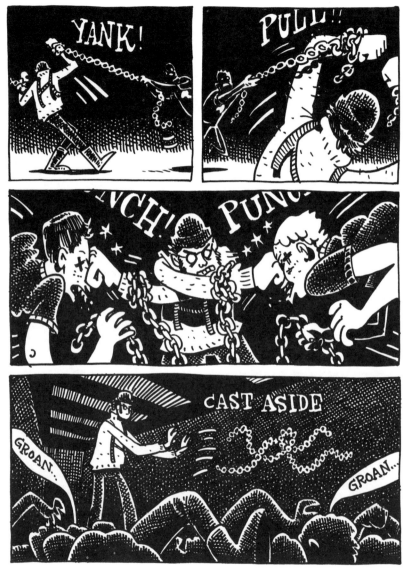

FLICKER BACK ON!
CHRIST, YOU'RE JUST KIDS!
GROAN
KOFF
WAIT, WEREN'T THERE THREE OF YOU?
BONK.

ROAN
WE NEED TO GO FASTER.
WHY? WHO'S CHASING US?
BARTY REDGRAVE AND MY HUSBAND...

"...BOTH CHASING AFTER THE SAME THING BESSEHL WANTS, NO DOUBT."
STRUGGLE!
STRUGGLE!
RELAX, SHANKS.
THIS WILL ALL GO A LOT SMOOTHER IF YOU'RE CALM.
B
TIGHTEN

LET ME OUT OF THESE STRAPS, BESSEHL.
I'M NOT ONE OF YOUR SCIENCE EXPERIMENTS!
OH, BUT YOU ARE, SHANKS...
...YOU ARE!
ROLL
LET'S START WITH SOME PRIMING, SHALL WE?
I WANT YOU TO THINK BACK TO OUR LITTLE SCRIMSHAW CLUB...
...REMEMBER?
E.B.

DO YOU REMEMBER HOW I WAS THE ONE WHO STARTED THE CLUB?
...HOW I WAS THE ONE WHO DID THE MOST RESEARCH, AND CONNECTED THE MOST DOTS?
I SHOULD HAVE BEEN ARCTAVIUS' CONFIDANT, SHANKS, NOT YOU!
JUST LOOK WHAT YOU DID WITH HIS CONFIDENCE, SHANKS...
HE TOLD YOU THE MAP TO FAR ARDEN AND YOU THREW IT AWAY!
THAT MAP SHOULD HAVE BEEN MINE, SHANKS, AND NOW I WANT YOU TO GIVE IT TO ME!

THIS IS IT. BOOTHIA COLLEGE. SHANKS AND AMBER MUST BE INSIDE.
BOOTHIA
ALRIGHT, LET'S GLIDE HER IN GENTLY.
ALISTAIR, HIT THAT LEVER TO DROP ANCHOR.
AYE, AYE!
DAVID, BRING IN ALL THE SHEETS EXCEPT THE MAIN ROYAL STAYSAIL AND THE MIZZEN TOPGALLANT STAYSAIL.
I'LL DO MY BEST!

OKAY...
OTHIA
LLEGE
...WE'VE STOPPED.
SHOULD I HELP YOU TIE OFF--
NO. GO FIND SHANKS AS FAST AS POSSIBLE.
OH, AND DAVID...?
AREOPA
DO BE CAREFUL.

LOOK, BESSEHL, I'D **LOVE** TO TELL YOU THE ROUTE TO FAR ARDEN, BUT I'VE LONG SINCE **FORGOTTEN** IT...
...AND THE ONLY HARD COPY OF THE MAP WAS ON MY SHIP, BUT THAT GOT **STOLEN**--
I **KNOW**, YOU IDIOT. ***I*** STOLE THE AREOPAGITICA --BUT THERE WAS NO MAP ON BOARD!
WELL, THEN, UNLESS YOU'RE PLANNING TO **DIG** INSIDE MY MIND AND **TEASE OUT** THAT FORGOTTEN MEMORY, YOU'RE OUT OF LUCK.
ACTUALLY, SHANKS...
...THAT'S **EXACTLY** WHAT I INTEND TO DO.

XI

AREOPAGITICA

I WISH I'D BEEN BORN TWO HUNDRED YEARS AGO, SHANKS, WHEN THE ARCTIC WAS KNOWN AS NOTHING MORE THAN...
...TERRA INCOGNITA.
I WAS DEVASTATED, SHANKS, WHEN YOU AND SIMON -- AND THE MAP -- WENT TO DIE ON EGLINTON ISLAND.

I THOUGHT: THERE GOES MY SHOT AT FILLING IN THE LAST BLANK SPOT ON THE GLOBE.
MY LAST CHANCE TO WALK IN THE BOOTS OF FRANKLIN, NANSEN ... HALL.
LIGHT
BUT THEN I HAD AN EPIPHANY, SHANKS.
I REALIZED THAT, WHILE NOT SOMETHING YOU CAN PLANT A FLAG IN ...
... THE BRAIN IS THE MOST INCREDIBLE TERRA INCOGNITA IN THE WORLD. A VAST CONTINENT UPON WHOSE SHORES ...

"...SCIENTISTS HAVE ONLY JUST RECENTLY STEPPED FOOT."
DRAG ASHORE
BOOTHIA
CAIRD II
RUN
RUN
BOOTHIA COLLEGE

BUT I WASN'T CONTENT WITH WAITING ON THAT METAPHORICAL SHORE.
I WANTED TO PUSH INLAND AS FAST AND AS FAR AS POSSIBLE.
TWIST!
I FORGED MY ROUTE BY STUDYING **MEMORY**. SPECIFICALLY, I LOOKED FOR PATTERNS AMONG THE **TRILLIONS** OF NEURAL PATHWAYS THAT EXIST BETWEEN OUR EARS.
I BELIEVED THEN, AS I DO NOW, THAT **MEMORIES** ARE NOTHING MORE...
PULL!
CRUNC
CRAC
BREA
...THAN **UNIQUE COMBI-NATIONS** OF THESE NEURAL CONNECTIONS. COMPLETELY **QUANTIFIABLE**!

BIOLOGY DEPT.
AMBER?
SHANKS?
GROAN
GROAN
WHERE'S AMBER?
YOU MEAN YOUR FAKE GIRLFRIEND?
BESSEHL ALREADY TOOK CARE OF HER.
SHE WASN'T FAKE!!
SOCK!!!

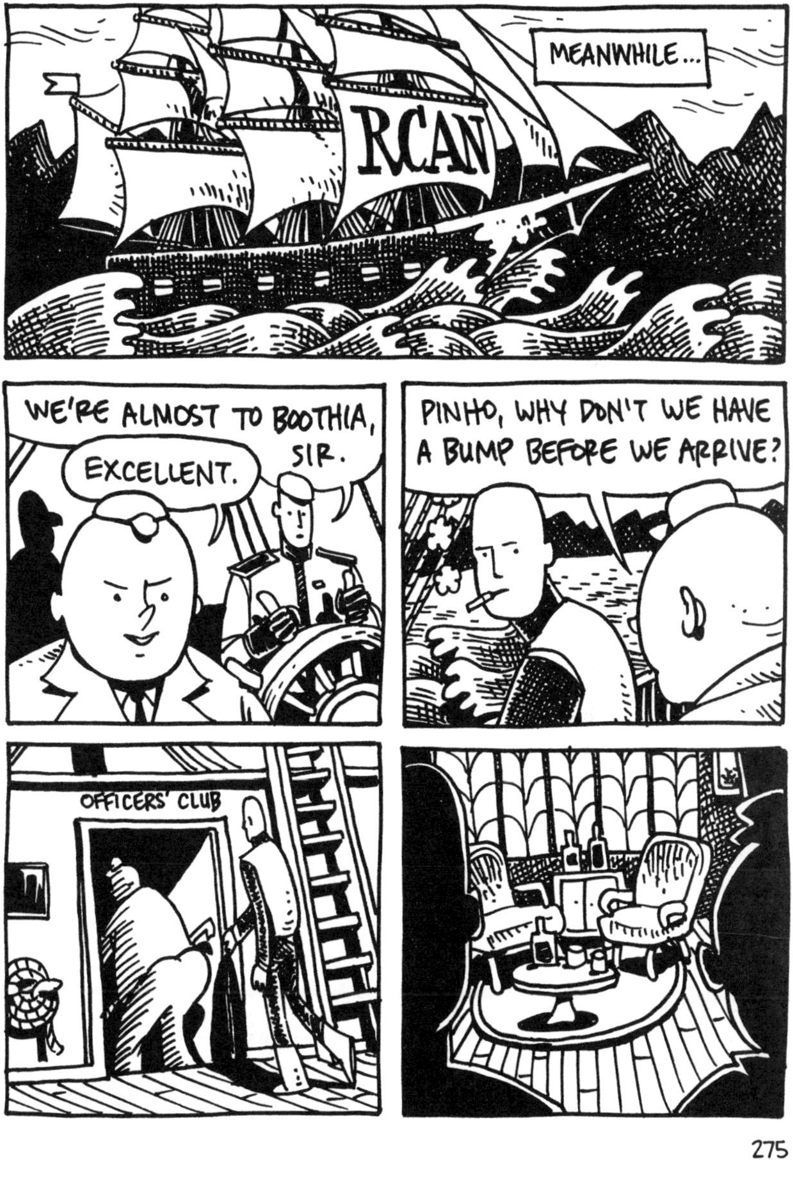
MEANWHILE...
RCAN
WE'RE ALMOST TO BOOTHIA, SIR.
EXCELLENT.
PINHO, WHY DON'T WE HAVE A BUMP BEFORE WE ARRIVE?
OFFICERS' CLUB

EVERYTHING ALRIGHT, BARTY?
CAN YOU BELIEVE SHANKS? THAT SNAKE!
WORKING WITH BESSEHL THIS WHOLE TIME, BEHIND OUR BACKS.
...AND YOUR WIFE WAS IN ON IT THE WHOLE TIME!
YES. WELL. THE THREE OF THEM WILL HAVE QUITE A SURPRISE WHEN WE SLIP INTO PASLEY BAY (WHERE BOOTHIA COLLEGE IS LOCATED) AND TAKE BACK THE AREOPAGITICA.
NOT SO FAST, PINHO...

..."I'VE GOT A BETTER IDEA."
MISS FORTUNA...
CAIRD II
...R-C-A-N IS GETTING CLOSER!
RCAN
GOOD. I CAN'T WAIT FOR YOU TO MEET MY HUSBAND, THE LATE ANTHONY PINHO.
LATE?
IS HE A GHOST?
NO...
...BUT AS FAR AS OUR MARRIAGE IS CONCERNED...

"...HE MAY AS WELL BE DEAD."
SHANKS, MAY I PROUDLY PRESENT TO YOU...
...THE deathMRI!!!
deathMRI
UNVEIL!!!

WHAT'S ALL THIS, THEN?
WHEN A PERSON DIES, SHANKS, THEIR BRAIN MAKES ONE LAST EXPLOSIVE CRY FOR HELP...
FOLD
...FIRING EVERY NEURAL CONNECTION AT ONCE, LIKE A NEURAL SUPERNOVA.
FOLD
IT'S WHAT SURVIVORS CALL THE WHITE LIGHT, AND IS MOST OFTEN INTERPRETED AS HEAVEN.
BUT THE WHITE LIGHT ISN'T A TUNNEL OR A PLACE...
...IT'S EVERY MEMORY YOU'VE EVER ACCUMULATED -- EVERY TASTE, EVERY SMELL, EVERY SIGHT...

...ALL COMING BACK TO YOU IN A FLASH.
POSSIBLY GIVING WAY
WHAT THIS MEANS FOR US, SHANKS, IS THAT IN A FEW MINUTES, WHEN I TAKE YOU TO THE EDGE OF DEATH...
...YOUR BRAIN'S NEURAL NETWORK WILL LIGHT UP, REVEALING--AMONG OTHER THINGS--THE MAP TO FAR ARDEN!
YOU, OF COURSE, WILL DIE IN THE PROCESS, BUT THAT'S NECESSARY FOR THE deathMRI TO LIVE UP TO ITS NAME.
NOW HOLD STILL, YOU MAY FEEL SOME PRESSURE.
TIGHTEN!

WE'RE NEARING THE AREOPAGITICA, SIR. PREPARE TO BOARD?
RCAN
RCAN
NO. CHANGE OF PLANS...
...READY THE CANNON!!
BARTY, ARE YOU OUT OF YOUR MIND? MY WIFE IS ON THAT SHIP!
CAPTAIN, I'M THE HIGHEST RANKING OFFICER ONBOARD AND I ORDER YOU TO STAND DOWN!
SORRY, MISTER PINHO, BUT ACCORDING TO THE BUREAU-CRACY...

"... YOU'RE A DEAD MAN."
PLEASE EXCUSE THE ENSUING SOLILOQUY, SHANKS, BUT I'M RATHER PROUD OF HER.
YOU SEE, I HAVE DEVISED A MACHINE THAT CAN PUSH A HUMAN BRAIN TO THAT SUPERNOVA STATE...
...AND THEN USING TECH-NOLOGY THAT IS MUCH TOO COMPLICATED TO EXPLAIN...
...THE deathMRI CAN CAPTURE THE EXPLOSION AND TRANSLATE THE DATA INTO A COMPREHENS-IBLE MEMORY MAP.
SO IN ESSENCE I'LL BE ABLE TO READ YOUR MIND!!

YGDALA
NEUROSCIENCE
WHAT'S YOUR EQ?
AMBER!
SHANKS!
RUN!
PRIVATE
...READ YOUR MI
BEE LINE
DAMMIT!
LOCKED!
AMBER! SHANKS!
POUND!
POUND!
POUND!
POUND!
POUND!
POUND!

SHANKS!!
deathMRI
DAVID!!
YOU CAN IGNORE HIM. I CHANGED THE LOCKS YESTERDAY.
WHY GET DAVID AND AMBER INVOLVED, ANYWAY? WHY THE WHOLE CHARADE?
I NEEDED YOU TO BE THINKING ABOUT THE FAR ARDEN MAP, TO HELP STRENGTHEN YOUR NEURAL CONNECTIONS.
AND I DEFINITELY NEEDED YOU TO NOT KNOW THAT I WAS BEHIND THIS...

"...BECAUSE A PERSON MAKES BETTER CONNECTIONS WHEN THEY'RE HAPPY."
TIE
THERE. JUST IN CASE A WAVE TRIES TO GOBBLE YOU UP.
YOU'RE NICE. I WISH YOU WERE MY MOM.
OH, I HOPE YOU MEAN THAT.
HUG!
FIRE!!
AREOPAGITICA
Shit.

AREOPAGIT

RUMBLE!!
FALL
WHA--?
PRIVATE
...AMBER?
PRIVATE

E.B.
CLICK
MI
ALRIGHT, LET'S SEE WHERE THAT MAP IS HIDING.
deathMRI
STRUGGLE
TA-TA, SHANKS.

LIGHTS FLICKER!!

HA, HA.
YOU'RE A LOT MORE VOCAL THAN MY PREVIOUS SUBJECT.
SHE JUST CLOSED HER EYES AND TOOK IT LIKE A--
BREAK IN!!
BOOTHIA
PRIVATE

DAMMIT.
LET'S BE A GOOD BOY, DAVID, AND--
SHUT DOWN!
TURN THE POWER BACK ON, DAVID! I'VE WAITED YEARS FOR THIS MOMENT!

SMASH
BOOTHIA
CLIMB IN!

XII

HOW COULD YOU?!
BOOTHIA
PUNCH!
WHUM
BOOTHIA

RCAN
RCAN
FORTUNA! FORTUNA!
WHAT WERE YOU THINKING? WHAT ABOUT FORTUNA?
YOUR WIFE DIED THREE YEARS AGO AS FAR AS I'M CONCERNED.

POP!
SCURRY!
GRAB!!
HEY!
I DID YOU A FAVOR, PINHO.
FORTUNA DOESN'T LOVE YOU. SHE LOVES SHANKS...
...SHE ALWAYS HAS.

AND FAR ARDEN? YOU JUST DESTROYED ANY HOPE OF FINDING IT.
GOOD.
NO PATCH OF LAND IS WORTH... THIS.
WE WERE A TEAM WHEN WE STARTED THE SCRIMSHAW CLUB, AND NOW LOOK AT US.
WHAT A WASTE.
GUARDS, LET HIM GO.
WIPE
RUB
GO FIND YOUR WIFE, PINHO.

JUMP!
RCA
DIVE!
SO DO YOU THINK BARTY FINALLY REALIZED THAT FAR ARDEN IS JUST A MYTH?
MORE LIKE HE FINALLY REALIZED THAT CHASING AFTER A FAIRY TALE WOULD HURT HIS POLL NUMBERS.
IF IT DOES EXIST, BETTER TO LET SOMEONE ELSE DO THE DIRTY WORK OF FINDING THE DAMN THING.
FULL SAIL BACK TOWARD DEVON, CAPTAIN...

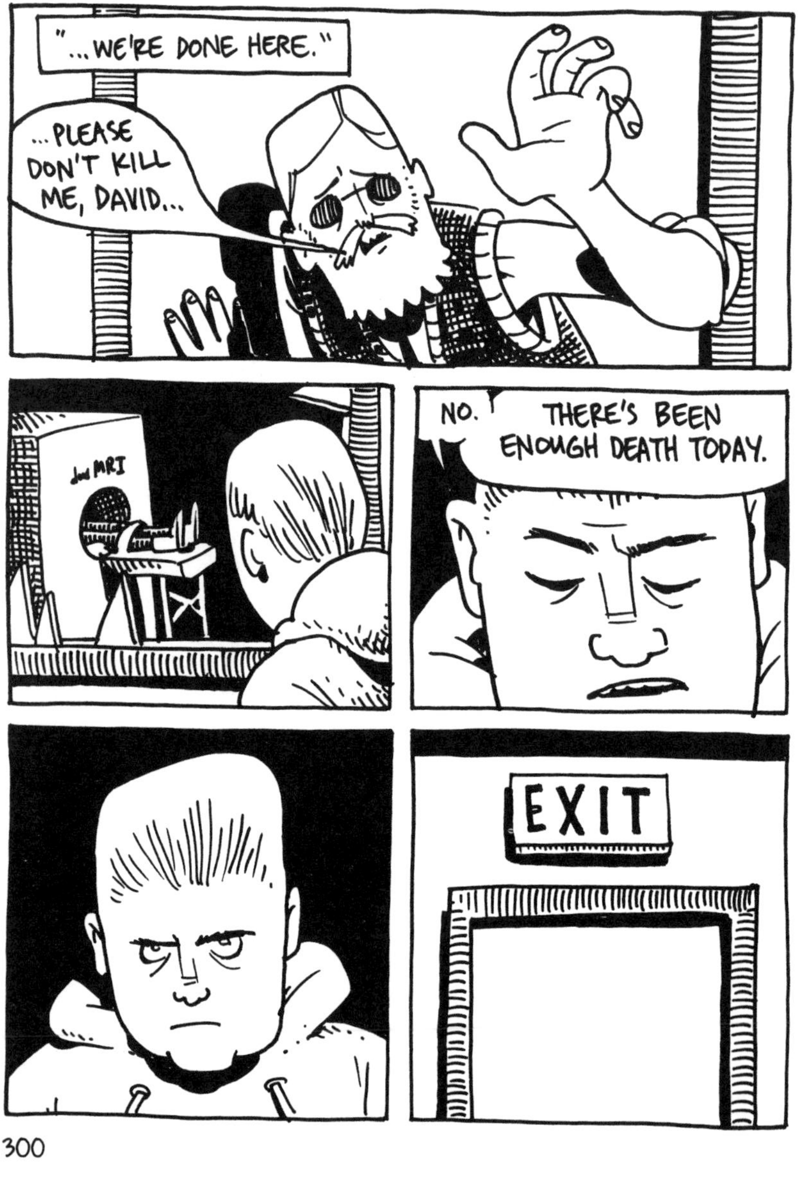
"...WE'RE DONE HERE."
...PLEASE DON'T KILL ME, DAVID...
MRI
NO.
THERE'S BEEN ENOUGH DEATH TODAY.
EXIT

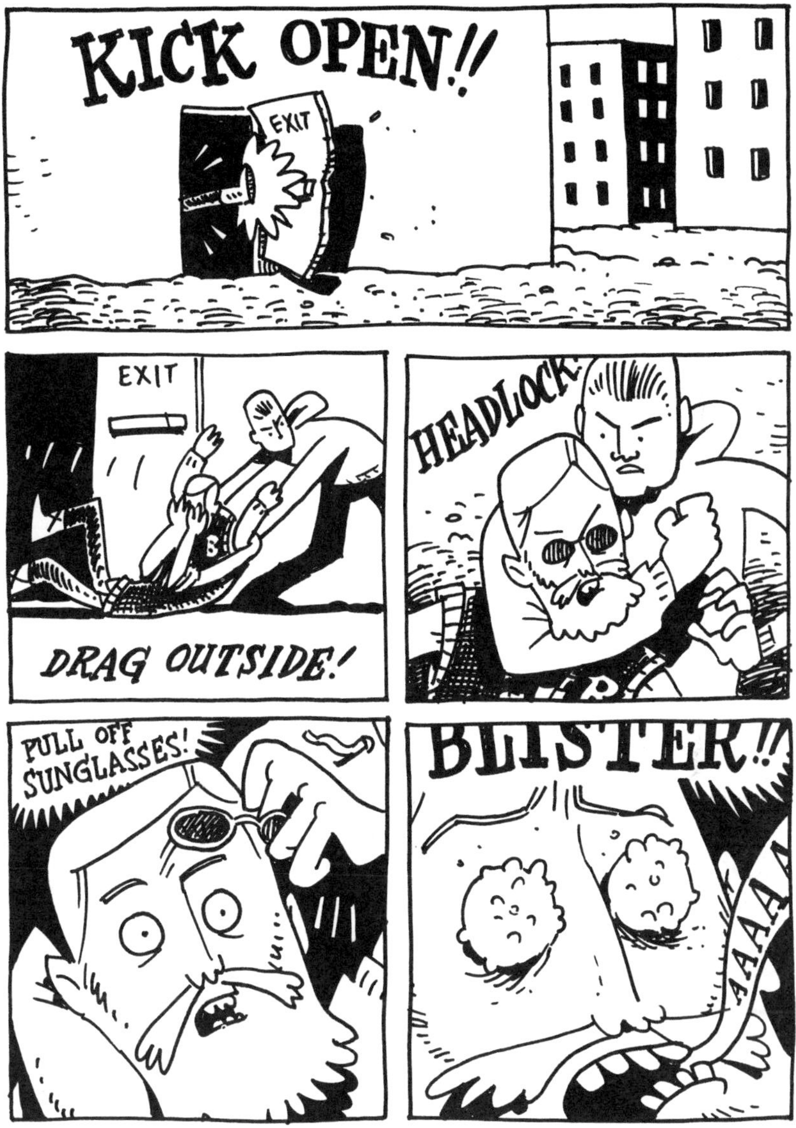
KICK OPEN!!
EXIT
EXIT
DRAG OUTSIDE!
HEADLOCK!
PULL OFF SUNGLASSES!
BLISTER!!
AAAAA

"...AAAAUUUGGGHHHHhhhhh..."

YOU WARMING UP, ALISTAIR?
IF IT WOULD HELP, I COULD GO INSIDE AND LOOK FOR MORE BLANKETS--
YOU'VE DONE ENOUGH.
HEY, FORTUNA, I DIDN'T BLOW UP THE AREOP--
HEY, LOOK.

BIOLOGY DEPT.
O2
ARMY...
PLEASE, BOTH OF YOU STAY HERE.

ARMY!
HUG!
IS HE OKAY, DAVID?
BOOTHI
HE'S ALIVE, ISN'T HE?

BOOTHIA
HEY, YOU WORK FOR THE NAVY, RIGHT?
UH... I USED TO.
WHY?
THERE'S A GIRL BACK THERE...
...SHE
OF COURSE. I'LL CALL THE HOSPITAL AND MAKE SURE HER FAMILY IS NOTIFIED.

BIOLOG
WALK INSIDE
I SCREWED UP, ALISTAIR.
HOODIE STRING PULL
DOES THIS MEAN WE'RE NOT GOING TO FAR ARDEN?
SOB!!

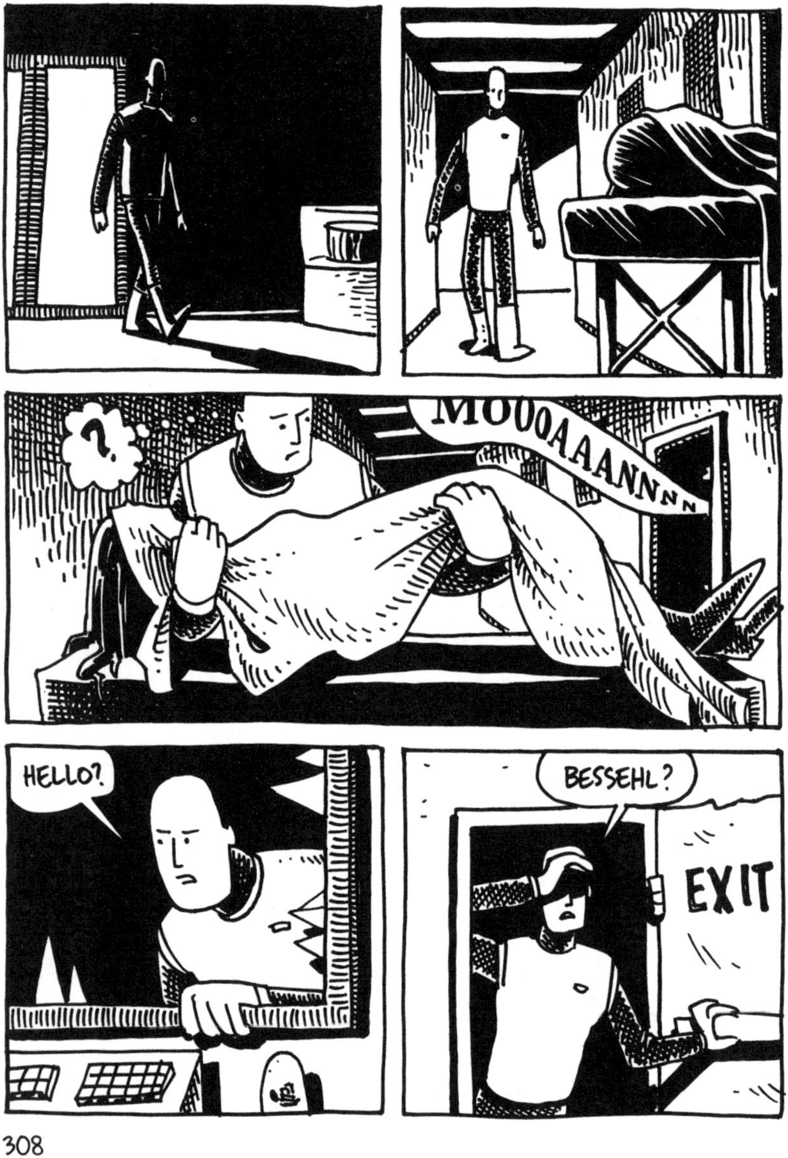
MOOOAAAANNNNN
HELLO?
BESSEHL?
EXIT

CRY CRY CRY
CRY CRY CRY CR
UH... I'M GOING TO GO FOR A WALK.
CRY CRY CRY
I'LL COME BACK WHEN EVERYONE'S HAPPY AGAIN.
♫
NEAT!
FOG!

PINHO? IS THAT YOU?
CHRIST, EMILE. LOOK AT YOU.
SHANKS! DID YOU SEE SHANKS? IS HE **DEAD**?
HE'S ALIVE, BESSEHL.
HA! THERE'S HOPE YET! BOYS, FIRE UP THE MAGNET!

PULL ASIDE
YOU'VE GOT TO GET HIM TO A HOSPITAL!
NO WAY! EVERY MOUNTIE IN NUNAVUT WILL BE LOOKING FOR HIM!
GESTICULATE
OKAY-- TAKE HIM TO THIS ADDRESS ON ELLESMERE. IT'S A BIG NORTH GREEN HIDEOUT. ASK FOR A GUY NAMED **HANDSOME JACK**.
TELL HIM I NEED ANOTHER FAVOR.

WAIT!
TURN AROUND
YOU SHOULD COME WITH US.
NO...
...I NEED TO MAKE THINGS RIGHT WITH MY WIFE.

♫ A WHOLE NEW WORLD... A NEW FANTASTIC POINT OF VIEW... ♫
♫... NO ONE TO TELL US NO, OR WHERE TO GO... ♫
♫ ... OR SAY WE'RE ONLY DRE-E-E-E-EAMING--
WHAT--?
HEY, YOU GUYS, **LOOK!** IT'S THAT **THING**...

...the Gold-Colored Narwhal!

HERE WE GO, YOUNG LADY. YOU--
BIOLOGY DEPT.
!
DOUBLE-TAKE!

3 DAYS LATER
ARMY? BABY? DO YOU KNOW WHERE YOU ARE?
O2
FISHSTICKS.
I'M GLAD YOU'RE **AWAKE**, AT LEAST.
KISS

HOW'S SHANKS?
BOOTH
DELUSIONAL.
Minsky
ARE YOU OKAY UP THERE, ALISTAIR?
BUT...
YEP! I STILL SEE THE NARWHAL.
...HOLD ON...
I THINK HE'S **POINTING** AT SOMETHING...

XIII

Meanwhile... (AT THE SOMBER MOOSE)
HE'S HERE.
THANKS FOR MEETING US HERE, MR. PINHO.
SURE. YOU'RE BARTY'S--
PINHO!
BY GOD, WE ALL THOUGHT YOU WAS DEAD!
HEY, I'VE STILL GOT A BOTTLE OF OUR "INVESTMENT" -- I'LL FIX UP YOU AND YER FRIENDS!

I HOPE YOU HAVE FOOD IN YOUR STOMACHS.
THERE Y'ARE.
YOU CAN KEEP THE BOTTLE, PINHO....
...BUT TELL **RCAN** THEY OWE ME 2,000 CANADIAN DOLLARS FOR TEARING MY BAR APART!
AND, UH, ANOTHER **500** FOR... "PSYCHO-LOGICAL TURMOIL."
HERE. THE ROYAL CANADIAN ARCTIC NAVY APOLOGIZES.
WOW!
MUCH ABLIGED, PINHO!

SNIFF
SNIFF
DRIN
SO... YOU'RE BARTY'S **ENTOURAGE**, RIGHT?
NOT EXACTLY.
ALLOW US TO GET RIGHT TO THE POINT.
WE BELIEVE THAT YOUR FRIEND, MR. SHANKS, IS IN **GRAVE DANGER**.
WHAT? WHY?
WE PULLED THIS OFF THE GIRL THAT BESSEHL KILLED THREE DAYS AGO.
DO YOU RECOGNIZE THIS DOCUMENT?
AUG
GAUAUUG

NO.
WE HAD RCAN'S BEST CRYPTOGRAPHER LOOK AT IT. TURNS OUT IT'S JUST A SIMPLE STRING OF RNA CODONS.
EVEN A TEENAGER WITH A GENETICS-THEMED GRAPHIC NOVEL COULD HAVE FIGURED THIS CODE OUT.
AUG
SO? WHAT DOES IT **SAY**?
"DIE SHANKS DIE."
THAT'S **IT**??
MR. PINHO, WE NEED YOUR HELP.
WE BELIEVE THAT MR. SHANKS' LIFE MAY BE THREATENED BY THE LETTER'S SENDER-- A MR. **SIMON ARCTAVIUS**.

LET ME SEE THAT.
THIS MUST BE A FORGERY FROM BESSEHL. SOME KIND OF **RUSE**.
OH?
HOW CAN YOU BE SO SURE?
ARCTAVIUS WOULD NEVER HURT SHANKS. HE WAS SHANKS' BEST FRIEND AND MENTOR.
BESIDES...

"... ARCTAVIUS PROBABLY DIED **YEARS AGO** ON HIS QUEST FOR FAR ARDEN."
GOOD KNOT, ALISTAIR.
ALISTAIR, ARMY IS AWAKE AND MAKING SENSE NOW. DO YOU WANT TO SEE HIM?
!
SCRAMB
BOOTHI

ARMY?
COME IN, ALISTAIR.
SIT
WE MADE IT.
YEAH, WE MADE IT.

ARMY, I, UH ... I KNOW THAT YOU'RE MY UNCLE.
AND I KNOW THAT YOU KILLED MY FOSTER DAD ...
... BUT ONLY BECAUSE HE KILLED MY REAL DAD -- YOUR BROTHER.
WHY DIDN'T YOU SAY ANY-THING? WHY DIDN'T YOU TELL ME THE WHOLE TRUTH RIGHT FROM THE BEGINNING?
ALISTAIR ...
SOMETIMES ADULTS KEEP THE TRUTH FROM KIDS UNTIL THE RIGHT MOMENT. IT'S TO PROTECT THE KIDS FROM CONFUSION ...

"...AND TO PROTECT THE ADULTS FROM SHAME."
CAN YOU BELIEVE WE'RE HERE?!
HERE, IN FAR AR--
GRUMBLE
ALI, WHAT'S WRONG?
ARMY THINKS I'M JUST A LITTLE KID.
KICK!

I'LL GO TALK TO HIM, OKAY?
YOU KNOW WHO NEVER ONCE LIED TO ME?
ME?
ANGER!
BOOTHIA
ANGER'S GONNA BE A BIG MOVIE STAR AND ADOPT ME AND ONLY TELL ME THE TRUTH ABOUT STUFF.
ANGER THE MAN-BEAST?
UH...

SUUUURE... I BET HE SURVIVED THAT **POLAR BEAR ATTACK** AND IS HALFWAY TO **VANCOUVER** BY NOW.
NOW C'MON. LET'S GET READY FOR THE TREK UP THIS RIDGE.
ACCORDING TO KINCAID, WE MAY RUN INTO SOME ANGRY RED-HEADED NORSEMEN.
HEY! I THOUGHT YOU DIDN'T BELIEVE KINCAID!
YEAH, WELL...
...I THREW **RATIONAL THINKING** OUT THE WINDOW ONCE WE STARTED FOLLOWING A GOLD-COLORED NARWHAL THROUGH THE FOG!
BOOTHIA

SHANKS.
FORTUNA.
Argh! We meet again, Shanks!!
HA HA, REMEMBER THAT ADVENTURE, ARMY?
C'MERE.
O_2

THOSE WERE GOOD TIMES.
THE BEST TIMES.
I THINK WHAT I REMEMBER MOST FONDLY IS YOU IN YOUR LITTLE BLACK SWIMSUIT.
THAT'S FUNNY...
...I DON'T REMEMBER BEING **IN** IT VERY OFTEN!

ALISTAIR NEEDS TO KNOW.
THAT YOU'RE HIS MOTHER.
I KNOW! I KNOW!
BUT HOW?
HOW AM I SUPPOSED TO TELL A KID THAT HE LIVED AT THE BEECHEY ORPHANAGE...
...WHILE HIS MOTHER WAS ACROSS WELLINGTON CHANNEL DOING SHOTS AT THE SOMBER MOOSE?

I'M A HORRIBLE HUMAN BEING!!
THAT'S TRUE.
DOUBLE-FIST PUNCH!!
JERK!
FIST CATC
FIST CATCH!
YOU **WERE** HORRIBLE...

...WHICH IS WHY YOU KNEW HE WAS BETTER OFF AT THE ORPHANAGE.
WIPE
BESIDES, YOU SENT HIM MONEY, TOYS, CLOTHES, FOOD--
PFFT. A BOY DOESN'T WANT CANS OF BEANS, HE WANTS HIS MOTHER.
CRAWL UNDER COVERS
THIS IS A REALLY SMALL BED.
I DON'T CARE.

O2
Hang in there Army! —Alister
I'M GOING TO MAKE THINGS RIGHT WITH ALISTAIR.
I KNOW YOU ARE.

NUZZLE
WE CAN START OVER HERE.
MM-HMM.
WILL YOU? LEAVE THAT HORRIBLE SHACK ON DEVON AND LIVE HERE WITH ALISTAIR AND ME?
OF COURSE.

GOOD CHOICE.
O_2
UNMASK
Time Passes, etc.
WHY DON'T YOU GET SOME REST, ARMY?
I'M GOING OUTSIDE NOW...

"...AND I MAY BE SOME TIME."
OATS?
CHECK.
PEMMICAN?
CHECK.
DANISH BUTTER?
YEP.
OKAY, IF THE WORST CASE HAPPENS AND THERE'S NOTHING UP THERE...
...AT LEAST WE'LL HAVE OURSELVES A FINE PICNIC LUNCH!
AGREED.
LET'S GO!!

WAIT, ISN'T SHANKS COMING?
HE'S STILL RECOVERING, DAVID. TOO WEAK FOR PHYSICAL ACTIVITY.
CAN YOU IMAGINE IF HE DIED ON THE HIKE UP THE RIDGE... BEFORE EVER SEEING FAR ARDEN?
...THAT'S THE DEFINITION OF TRAGEDY.

DAVID'S WORRIED THAT WE MIGHT GET ATTACKED!
AND HE WANTS ARMY TO PROTECT HIM!
HA HA
HA HA
YOU KNOW, THERE MIGHT NOT EVEN BE ANYTHING ON THE ISLAND.
IT MIGHT JUST BE A WASTELAND!
OH, C'MON.
ALISTAIR WAS ONLY JOKING.

YEAH... I KNOW.
ALMOST THERE!
CLIMB!!
I WANT TO BE FIRST!

RUN!
BARK!
BARK!
BARK!
RETURN

PICK!
SUCCULENT BITE!
HEAVEN...
...SIMPLY HEAVEN...
NOTICE!

ANGER!
PULL
YOU'RE ALIVE!!
RUNNING HUG!

OF COURSE I'M ALIVE! I COULDN'T LET THAT POLAR BEAR WIN!
I BET YOU CLOBBERED HIM!
HA, HA -- HE DIDN'T EVEN KNOW WHAT HIT HIM!
YAY!
I'LL TELL YOU ALL ABOUT IT IN THE FOREST.
C'MON!
IN THERE?
OKAY.

Minsky

SNORE...
ARMY?
SQUINT
NO, IT CAN'T BE...

SIMON!!
YOU'RE A LITTLE LATE, WOULDN'T YOU SAY?

BETTER LATE THAN NEVER, RIGHT?
SPEAKING OF **LATE**, SORRY I DIDN'T COME DOWN TO MEET YOU WHEN YOU DOCKED.
I WAS EXPECTING YOU TO ARRIVE IN THE **AREOPAGITICA** ...NOT THIS PIECE OF CRAP.
KNOCK KNOC!
WHAT IS THIS, **PINE**?
IT'S GOOD TO SEE YOU AGAIN, SIMON. YOU HAVEN'T CHANGED A BIT.
YOU TOO, ARMY.
HAND-SHAKE!

DAVID?
SCRAMBLE
AMBER?

BUT YOU'RE **DEAD**.
I NEVER **DIED**, SILLY. I'VE BEEN HERE THE WHOLE TIME!
OH, WE'RE GOING TO HAVE SUCH A **WONDERFUL LIFE** HERE!
HUG!

WHERE ARE WE GOING?
TUG
JUST INSIDE THE FOREST. YOU'LL LOVE IT THERE.
SOMETHING'S WRONG HERE, CAN'T YOU FEEL IT?
CAN'T YOU TURN YOUR STUPID BRAIN OFF FOR ONE MINUTE?!
LOOK, I'LL ANSWER ALL YOUR QUESTIONS IN THE FOREST, OKAY?

CHEW
CHEW
CHEW
CHE
CHEW
CHEW
CHEW
YOU SAY... I'LL UNDERSTAND EVERYTHING ONCE I'M IN THE FOREST?
YEP.
BUT IT'S SO DARK IN THERE.
DON'T WORRY, DAVID...

"... YOUR EYES WILL ADJUST."
...AND THAT'S HOW I BEFRIENDED THE NORSE TRIBE AND BECAME THEIR KING.
FASCINATING!
NOW COME ON, I WANT YOU TO MEET EVERYONE.
YEAH, I'D LIKE THAT!
JUST LET ME PUT MY OXYGEN MASK ON.

YOU DON'T NEED THAT. JUST COME WITH ME.
HA, HA. I'M NOT THE WIRE-THIN RIGHAND I ONCE WAS, SIMON.
YOU'RE **FINE**, SHANKS.
YOU DON'T **NEED** THE OXYGEN.
CALM **DOWN**, SIMON, YOU--
SIMON?

SIMON?

GET UP!

PANT!
PANT!
PANT

SIMON?
Minskg
SIMO
SIMON?
SIMON--
JESUS...

FORTUNA!
CONVULSE
CONVULSE
FORTUNA
COME ON. GET UP.
LIFT!!

DAVID!
CONVULSE! CONVULSE!
LIFT!

WHERE'S...
WHERE'S...
TWITCH

SOON...
HANG ON, ALISTAIR.
WE'RE ALMOST TO THE BOAT.
NOTICE!

EPILOGUE

Later, at the Ice Palace...
WE NEED TO ASK YOU A FEW QUESTIONS, MR. SHANKS.
Ice Palace

JUST A FORMALITY, REALLY.
SO WE CAN CLOSE OUR CASE.
THAT'S FINE.
THE YOUNG MAN-- DAVID-- DO YOU KNOW WHAT HIS LAST NAME WAS?
NO.
THE WOMAN-- FORTUNA. WE UNDERSTAND SHE'D BEEN IN HIDING FOR THREE YEARS?

YES.
CAN I GO NOW?
NOT YET.
DOES SHE HAVE ANY FAMILY IN THE AREA?
NO. JUST PINHO. HER HUSBAND.
HE WAS IN HIDING AS WELL.
ALRIGHT.
AND...
THE BOY.
HE WAS YOUR NEPHEW?

YES.
WHAT WAS HIS FULL NAME?
FOR THE RECORD.
ALISTAIR CAVENDISH.
IF IT'S ANY CONSOLATION, MR. SHANKS--
WE'RE NOT 100% SURE WHAT KIND OF GAS WAS SPEWING FROM THAT ISLAND--
--BUT IN CASES LIKE THESE, THE VICTIMS GENERALLY DIE VERY PEACEFULLY.
A KIND OF PRE-DEATH EUPHORIA.

ANYWAY.
OH, ONE LAST THING, MR. SHANKS.
THIS BOX CONTAINS THE ITEMS ON FORTUNA'S PERSON.
THIS SHOULD LEGALLY GO TO PINHO, BUT--OFF THE RECORD--WE FEEL THAT YOU SHOULD HAVE IT.
TUCK IN POCKET
AREN'T YOU GOING TO OPEN IT?
I KNOW WHAT'S INSIDE.

SHANKS!!
THE END OF ANOTHER BIG ADVENTURE FOR OL' SHANKS!
HOW DO YOU FEEL, ARMY?
HUNGRY.
HA HA! YOU WOULDN'T BELIEVE THE PRESS WE'RE GETTING!
"Devon Islander Finds Far Arden--colon--Death Trap!"

GO AWAY, BARTY.
WHERE'RE YOU GOING, SHANKS? CBC INTERVIEW?
THE KITCHEN, BARTY. GET LOST.
OH! I FORGOT THE BEST PART! I FOUND A SCIENTIST WHO'LL SAY THAT THE FAR ARDEN GAS IS CAUSING GLOBAL WARMING!
WITH A HOOK LIKE THAT I COULD MANEUVER MY WAY ONTO THE HIGH ARCTIC LEAGUE!
?
KITCHEN
SHUT FIRMLY!
THE HIGH ARCTIC LEAGUE!

THERE YOU ARE.

SNIFF
SHRUG.
OPEN

Alistair's
FAMOUS
PIPE TOBACCO
Rich
CAVENDISH
flavour!
G
!
BARK!
BARK!
BARK!
BARK!
OH.
HEY, BUDDY.

END.

Thanks so much to Chris Staros, Brett Warnock, Leigh Walton, and Rob Venditti at Top Shelf Productions for believing in this book.

And special thanks to all those who supported Far Arden during its bizarre online serialization, especially (but definitely not limited to): Steven Stwalley, Zander Cannon, Tom Spurgeon, my parents, and everyone at the Minneapolis Cartoonist Conspiracy.

Most of all, thanks to Sam Fellman for so enthusiastically sharing your interest in polar exploration all those years ago.

KEVIN CANNON LIVES IN THE NEAR-ARCTIC CLIMES OF MINNEAPOLIS, MINNESOTA.

HE SPENDS HIS DAYS ILLUSTRATING NONFICTION GRAPHIC NOVELS WITH ZANDER CANNON (NO RELATION). NOTABLE TITLES INCLUDE *BONE SHARPS, COWBOYS, AND THUNDER LIZARDS* (2005), *THE STUFF OF LIFE: A GRAPHIC GUIDE TO GENETICS AND DNA* (2009), AND *T-MINUS: THE RACE TO THE MOON* (2009).